"Bobby Jamieson's *The Path to Bei...* ...izes the experience of becoming a pastor, and the process of decision-making surrounding it. For those wrestling with whether to pursue the pastorate, *The Path to Being a Pastor* will be both an encouraging and thought-provoking read, and will give them biblical, practical, and edifying steps for how to move forward. Give this excellent book both to aspiring pastors and to current pastors who seek to encourage them."

Gavin Ortlund, Senior Pastor, First Baptist Church of Ojai; author, *Finding the Right Hills to Die On*

"This is a gold mine of pastoral wisdom filled with answers to questions we all ask, as well as answers to questions we should ask. I have been a pastor for fifteen years and I learned something in every chapter. If you are considering pastoral ministry, this book is a gift to you."

Andrew Wilson, Teaching Pastor, King's Church London

"This clear-thinking and realistic book covers all the essential matters that a man considering pastoral ministry ought to ponder. I appreciated not only the biblical comprehensiveness but also the very practical rootedness in the actual life of churches. This will be an accessible and useful resource for a man to work through slowly, perhaps with his wife and a group of trusted friends. Jamieson is a sure-footed, measured, and well-informed guide."

Christopher Ash, Writer in Residence, Tyndale House, Cambridge

"Bobby Jamieson is a gift to the church, as is *The Path to Being a Pastor*. I heartily recommend this book for all who are contemplating a life of ministry service and for seasoned ministers who are shepherding along these conversations."

Jason K. Allen, President, Midwestern Baptist Theological Seminary

"Bobby Jamieson writes with wisdom beyond his years as he tackles some of the most pressing questions men wrestle with as they consider becoming an elder. He is careful to distinguish between revealed truth and matters of prudence, which makes this book a unique gift in the field, reaching beyond typical cultural limitations. I cannot wait to get this into the hands of prospective elders here in Canada. Written from a humble and generous heart, *The Path to Being a Pastor* fills an important void in the current literature. I am so thankful he took the time to write it."

Paul Martin, Senior Pastor, Grace Fellowship Church, Toronto, Canada

"For most young men, the path to being a pastor is simply to go to seminary and then try to get hired. I can only imagine how much good it will do for many pastors and churches if they would carefully consider what Bobby Jamison lays out as 'the path to being a pastor.' This book will challenge and stretch you, and at times might overwhelm you. But most certainly, it will be a great help for those who aspire to be pastors."

Matthias Lohmann, Chairman, Evangelium21; Pastor, Free Evangelical Church Munich-Central, Germany

"This is a biblically accurate, very insightful, and practical book. In essence, it is a road map for becoming a faithful, fruitful, and blessed shepherd. It will also be a good tool in the training of new ministers."

Yevgeny Bakhmutsky, Pastor, Russian Bible Church, Moscow, Russia

"This is a helpful book, not just for those who are aspiring to be in pastoral ministry but also for those who are involved in the ministry of training young men aspiring to be in ministry. Thank you for demystifying the 'call to ministry,' which certainly plagues the churches in my part of the world and inevitably leads to many unbiblical misconceptions about pastoral ministry and ends up hurting the church in the process. In spite of many Western cultural references, it will serve the church in the East well to help prepare workers for ministry. I know that I will be using this book a lot!"

Hezekiah Harshit Singh, Pastor, Satya Vachan Church, Lucknow, India

"Biblically sound, pastorally wise, and pointedly practical, *The Path to Being a Pastor* is eminently helpful for both would-be pastors and pastors alike. This will be at the top of my list of recommended books for anyone aspiring to pastoral ministry. It will also be required reading for all the interns at my church!"

Eugene Low, Lead Teaching Pastor, Grace Baptist Church, Singapore

The Path to Being a Pastor

The Path to Being
a Pastor

A Guide for the Aspiring

Bobby Jamieson

WHEATON, ILLINOIS

The Path to Being a Pastor: A Guide for the Aspiring

Copyright © 2021 by Robert Bruce Jamieson III

Published by Crossway
   1300 Crescent Street
   Wheaton, Illinois 60187

Cover design: Lindy Martin, Faceout Studios

Cover image: Shutterstock

First printing 2021

Printed in the United States of America

Trade paperback ISBN: 978-1-4335-7665-2
ePub ISBN: 978-1-4335-7668-3
PDF ISBN: 978-1-4335-7666-9
Mobipocket ISBN: 978-1-4335-7667-6

Library of Congress Cataloging-in-Publication Data

Names: Jamieson, Bobby, 1986– author.
Title: The path to being a pastor : a guide for the aspiring / Bobby Jamieson.
Description: Wheaton, Illinois: Crossway, 2021. | Series: 9Marks | Includes bibliographical references and index.
Identifiers: LCCN 2020049342 (print) | LCCN 2020049343 (ebook) | ISBN 9781433576652 (trade paperback) | ISBN 9781433576669 (pdf) | ISBN 9781433576676 (mobipocket) | ISBN 9781433576683 (epub)
Subjects: LCSH: Vocation, Ecclesiastical. | Vocation (in religious orders, congregations, etc.) | Clergy—Appointment, call, and election. | Pastoral theology.
Classification: LCC BV4011.4 .J36 2021 (print) | LCC BV4011.4 (ebook) | DDC 253/.2—dc23
LC record available at https://lccn.loc.gov/2020049342
LC ebook record available at https://lccn.loc.gov/2020049343

Crossway is a publishing ministry of Good News Publishers.

LB   30 29 28 27 26 25 24 23 22
15 14 13 12 11 10 9 8 7 6 5 4 3 2

To Isaac Adams

*"I love a minister whose face
invites me to make him my friend—
a man upon whose doorstep you read, 'Salve,' 'Welcome.'"*

CHARLES SPURGEON

Contents

Preface

LET'S BEGIN WITH HOW I am evidently unqualified to write this book. The title is *The Path to Being a Pastor*, and I am not *the* pastor of a church. I aspire to be a senior pastor, but that remains an aspiration. I have not yet completed the path that this book maps. If that breaks the deal for you, I understand. I will not be offended if you put this book back on the shelf or, more likely, close the Amazon preview window. I wish you all the best.

But, if you're still with me, here are two factors that temper my lack of ethos. First, though I am not *the* pastor of my church, I am *a* pastor. And I spend a decent chunk of my time mentoring men who aspire to be pastors. Here at Capitol Hill Baptist Church, we run a full-time pastoral internship. Every year, we host two classes of about six men each for an intense five-month residency. Our interns study ecclesiology and observe the church in order to gain a biblical framework and living model for pastoring. I oversee this internship, so I have conversations almost every day about the topics this book addresses. If you talk about something enough, writing a book about it just might save you time in the long run.

Second, though I haven't been a pastor very long, I have spent an inordinate amount of time preparing to pastor. At this point, I have spent far longer preparing to pastor than I have pastoring, roughly eleven years to three. Not the most impressive credential, I know.

But along the way, I have learned a few things, especially from godly friends walking the same path, whether alongside or ahead of me. I am trying to pass on a few lessons while they're fresh.

Like our church's internship, this book is for men who aspire to be pastors. I say "men" because the Bible does (1 Tim. 2:12). And the men I chiefly have in mind are those who desire to vocationally serve a local church as that church's primary preacher. Not all churches can afford to pay a pastor; some churches can pay more than one. And certainly, there are many roles—missions, student evangelism, counseling, writing, and more—that might broadly be considered full-time Christian ministry. The further your goal is from serving as a full-time preaching pastor, the less relevant this book will be. But if you want to be a senior pastor, you're in the bull's-eye.

In a sense, I am writing this book to myself of fourteen years ago, when I first began to think seriously about becoming a pastor. I was nineteen. In the previous few months, my heart had been gripped by the preaching of God's word by John MacArthur and the other pastors of Grace Community Church in Sun Valley, California. Though I was then seriously pursuing a vocation in music, a desire to preach and pastor full-time took root in my heart quickly and deeply. God's word preached was thoroughly remaking me, and I yearned to be an instrument of that renovating work in others' lives.

Is that your longing too? This book seeks to help guide that desire from seed to fruition. One of the main lessons is: it can take a while. So give yourself to cultivating gifts and godliness, and leave fruit to God.

This book is mainly counsel. It is mainly advice, an effort to apply Scripture to your life and mine. Each chapter is titled with and driven by an imperative. Sometimes that imperative comes straight from Scripture; sometimes it's my best effort to distill and deploy the sense of Scripture. In the latter case, I usually state the imperative starkly, but its smooth exterior hides a host of exceptions. I will try to point out those exceptions as they come, but consider this a blanket qualification. There is a lot of advice in this book. I don't dream that it all applies to every person and circumstance. Your mileage may vary; think Proverbs, not case law.

This book's goal is modest. To switch metaphors from path to house, I aim only to conduct a brief tour: to open doors, flick on lights, and point out some crucial features. I won't even get to every room in the house. (No chapter on evangelism!) I am only trying to get you started and help you get your bearings. My goal is to provoke you. I want to provoke you to study Scripture, examine yourself, pray, and seek counsel, especially from your church's pastors. Speaking of provoking you, the meddling starts in the first chapter.

Acknowledgments

IN MY OTHER BOOKS, I save the best for last, thanking my wife at the very end of the acknowledgements. But in this case, the book was as much her idea as mine. So thank you, Kristin, for what I, at least, think was a good idea. Thanks even more for reading the whole book as it came and for your heartening enthusiasm for what I wrote. And thanks most of all for being a sterling partner in life and ministry for the past twelve years.

In early 2020, I sketched the table of contents and wrote the preface, hoping to squeeze writing into the margins of ministry. Then the world stopped. So thank you, Mark Dever, for gladly supporting my writing this book during the sad, slow months when our church could not meet. And thank you for being a source and exemplar of so much of the good that this book attempts to commend.

I am thankful to Jonathan Leeman for making 9Marks a partner in this book's publication, and to Justin Taylor for gladly giving it a home at Crossway. Hearty thanks are also due to Kevin Emmert for his skillful editing. Trent Jones and John Lee deserve special thanks for vigorously encouraging the book when it was just an idea, and for reading the manuscript and offering insightful feedback. Jonathan Keisling and Drew Allenspach also read the whole thing and offered thoughtful comments, as did the Fall 2020 intern class of Capitol Hill Baptist Church. Thank you all.

ACKNOWLEDGMENTS

Warm thanks to friends whose counsel and wisdom enrich the following pages: Brian Bunnell, Chase Sears, Michael Lawrence, Tom Schreiner, and Isaac Adams. Finally, I thank the other pastors who have not yet been named here but who generously, graciously guided my path to being a pastor: Rick Holland, Greg Gilbert, Steve Auld, and Julian Hardyman.

PART 1

————————

FINDING THE PATH

1

Say "I Aspire," Not "I'm Called"

The saying is trustworthy: If anyone aspires to
the office of overseer, he desires a noble task.

1 TIMOTHY 3:1

HAVE YOU BEEN DROPPED into an existential crisis? A year or two ago, becoming a pastor was the farthest thing from your mind. You were contentedly working as a schoolteacher or studying to be an engineer. But then something happened. It might have been a sermon you heard or a conversation you had. A thought floated over the horizon of your mind: maybe you should be a pastor. In recent months, that little thought-cloud has quietly expanded. It now blankets your daily work, your plans, and your thoughts of the future. The more you think about pastoring, the more you want to do it. But how can you decide whether you should?

Most likely, you have picked up from Christians around you the vocabulary of *calling*. You are asking yourself, "Am I called to ministry?"

When a man who is not yet a pastor says he is called to be a pastor, he usually means something like this: "I have a constraining, settled, deeply rooted desire to serve full-time as a pastor." Those who speak this way are doing their best to put words to an intense, sobering experience. I share the experience and sympathize with the effort. Nevertheless, I am convinced that the language of "calling to ministry" points the whole conversation in the wrong direction. In this chapter, I aim to persuade you to set aside the language of *calling* and replace it with *aspiration*, specifically, aspiring to the office of elder, with the further aspiration of serving as an elder full-time. Instead of saying "I'm called to ministry," say "I aspire to be a pastor."[1]

My goal is for you to trade in the question, Am I called? in exchange for two different questions. First: Are you qualified to serve as an elder? Second: Should serving as an elder be your job? In pursuit of this goal, this chapter will identify two presumptions in saying that you are called to ministry, discuss two problems inherent in the language of calling, and commend five advantages of saying, instead, that you aspire to pastor.

Before we embark, I should underscore that as much as I care about the language we use, I care far more about the heart posture behind that language. Many thoughtful Christians use the language of calling to pastoral ministry, and I agree with much of what they mean. For instance, the Presbyterian Church in America's *Book of Church Order* says, "Ordinary vocation to office in the Church is the calling of God by the Spirit, through the inward testimony of a good conscience, the manifest approbation of God's people, and the concurring judgment of a lawful court of the Church."[2] I will register some disagreements

---

1 I first explored some of the ideas in this chapter in my article entitled "The Double Presumption of Calling to Ministry," 9Marks, August 24, 2014, https://www.9marks .org/article/the-double-presumption-of-calling-to-ministry/. I redeploy some of those ideas here in thoroughly reworked form.

2 *The Book of Church Order of the Presbyterian Church in America* (The Office of the Stated Clerk of the General Assembly of the Presbyterian Church in America,

with this below. But if you are committed to the language of calling, you could still agree with every word of the remaining chapters of this book. You could also agree about some of the pitfalls that lurk in the neighborhood of calling, which we will come to shortly.

The Double Presumption of "Calling" to Ministry

The expression "I'm called to ministry" asserts something about both God and yourself. You mean that, as far as you can tell, God is calling you to pastoral ministry. You think it is his will that you become a pastor. But you are also saying something about yourself. Generally, you are saying that you desire to be a pastor. More than that, you are saying you have a sense that you should be a pastor—as opposed to, say, a gardener or graphic designer. For those claims to make sense, you must think you are qualified to be a pastor, or at least well on your way.

More specifically, I want to argue that the phrase "I'm called to pastor" is pregnant with a double presumption. Saying that you are called to ministry presumes that, first, you are, or soon will be, qualified to be an elder; second, you are, or soon will be, sufficiently gifted in pastoral ministry that a church should pay you to do it. I call these presumptions not because the evidence necessarily contradicts them, but because saying so does not make it so. Let's consider each.

First, to say "I'm called to pastor" presumes that you are, or soon will be, qualified to serve as an elder of a local church. "Elder" is the term the New Testament most frequently uses for the office of teaching, shepherding, and pastoral oversight (e.g., Acts 14:23; 20:17; 1 Tim. 5:17; Titus 1:5; James 5:14; 1 Pet. 5:1). Less frequently, the New Testament

---

2019), 16–1. Available at https://www.pcaac.org/wp-content/uploads/2019/10/BCO-2019-with-bookmarks-for-website-1.pdf.

names this office "overseer" (Acts 20:28; 1 Tim. 3:2; Titus 1:7). The New Testament uses the noun "shepherd," also commonly rendered "pastor," with reference to the church office of pastor only once (Eph. 4:11). Both times the noun's verbal equivalent is used, elders are the ones who are charged to pastor, or "shepherd" (Acts 20:17, 28; 1 Pet. 5:1–2). In other words, the New Testament uses "elder," "overseer," and "pastor" interchangeably to name one office.[3] To be a pastor is to fulfill the office of elder. Every pastor is an elder, and every elder pastors.

Scripture tells us what kind of man an elder must be (1 Tim. 3:1–7; Titus 1:5–9; cf. 1 Pet. 5:1–5). If you want to pastor, you must meet those qualifications, which we will consider in chapter 3. If God is "calling" you to pastoral ministry, he will qualify you for that ministry. If you never meet the qualifications for eldership, then you are never called to be a pastor.

Second, saying you are called to pastor presumes that you are, or soon will be, sufficiently gifted in pastoral ministry that a church should pay you to do it. The New Testament requires that churches pay at least some of their pastors. In Galatians 6:6, Paul writes, "Let the one who is taught the word share all good things with the one who teaches." And in 1 Timothy 5:17–18, he says, "Let the elders who rule well be considered worthy of double honor, especially those who labor in preaching and teaching. For the Scripture says, 'You shall not muzzle an ox when it treads out the grain,' and, 'The laborer deserves his wages.'"

The basic principle is that eldering is hard work. Teaching God's word publicly is hard work. And while every elder must be able to

---

3 For a brief treatment of the New Testament's interchangeable use of "elder," "overseer," and "pastor," see Benjamin L. Merkle, "The Scriptural Basis for Elders," in *Baptist Foundations: Church Government for an Anti-Institutional Age*, ed. Mark Dever and Jonathan Leeman (Nashville, TN: B&H Academic, 2015), 243–52.

teach (1 Tim. 3:2), some elders will be especially gifted to teach, and will especially give themselves to teaching (1 Tim. 5:17). The whole church benefits from that teaching, and a man can do it best by giving it his best. So the church should relieve such men of the burden of providing for themselves by other means.

But this obligation to pay pastors does not mean churches should limit the number of their elders to those whom they can support financially. Some elders will be paid to serve full-time; others will not. In Acts 20:34–35, Paul reminds the elders of the church in Ephesus, "You yourselves know that these hands ministered to my necessities and to those who were with me. In all things I have shown you that by working hard in this way we must help the weak and remember the words of the Lord Jesus, how he himself said, 'It is more blessed to give than to receive.'" Here Paul invokes his example of working to provide for his own and others' needs as a model for these elders to follow. He clearly assumes that not all of them will be paid by the church. Throughout the New Testament, when elders of a church are mentioned, they consistently show up in the plural (Acts 14:23; Phil. 1:1; 1 Tim. 5:17; Titus 1:5; James 5:14; 1 Pet. 5:1). Where multiple men in a congregation are qualified to serve as elders, a church should have more than one.

Putting these passages together, we can say that each church should have multiple elders, and each church should financially support elders who devote themselves to public teaching, but not every elder will necessarily be paid by the church. Which means that you can be an elder without it being what provides your paycheck.

This has at least two implications for your "calling" or desire to be a pastor. First, distinguishing between serving as an elder and being paid for it clarifies what is at stake. Are you a sufficiently gifted preacher of God's word that a church should pay you to preach? The New Testament ties financial compensation for pastoral work to special labor in teaching, which assumes special ability in teaching (1 Tim. 5:17–18; Gal. 6:6). How gifted a preacher are you? What does your track record so far show? None of this implies that a church should not set aside pastors to serve full-time whose gifts are more pronounced in, say, counseling or evangelism. But most churches can afford to pay only one pastor, if that. And when they can hire only one pastor, they hire a preacher.

Second, aspiring to elder and aspiring to serve as a full-time preaching pastor are distinct. Biblically speaking, all elders are pastors. However, eldering is a broader category than full-time pastoring. To be a full-time preaching pastor is to occupy a subset of a broader office.

This distinction is freeing. Pastoring is not all-or-nothing. You are not limited to the two options of no pastoral ministry versus serving as a preaching pastor. Whether you will ever serve as an elder and whether that service will be your job are different matters.

There are two questions here, and it helps to keep them apart. Distinguishing the question of serving as an elder from what you do for your job can relieve some of the existential angst you may be feeling. It might be that your desire to help people grow spiritually suggests not that you should quit your job and move to seminary, but that you should aspire to eldership while keeping your job. If you desire to serve a local church as a pastor and teacher of God's word, then strive to meet these qualifications, start doing the work now as God enables, and entrust every aspect of your future to him.

Two Problems with Calling

Before saying more about this positive vision of aspiring to eldership, there are two problems with calling language that we should address. These two problems are exegesis and entitlement.

First, the exegetical problem is that the Bible does not use calling language to mean what we mean. The New Testament frequently uses "called" to describe God's effectual act of bringing us to saving faith (e.g., Rom. 1:6–7; 8:30; 9:24; 1 Cor. 1:9, 24; Gal. 1:6). The New Testament also uses "calling" to describe the life of holiness to which God has summoned us and for which God has empowered us through the gospel (Eph. 4:1; 1 Thess. 4:3–7). But nowhere does the New Testament use the verb "call" to describe God's act of assigning us a vocation, pastoral or otherwise. The closest the Bible comes to this is in 1 Corinthians 7:17: "Only let each person lead the life that the Lord has assigned to him, and to which God has called him." Paul then instructs Christians under various obligations not to seek release from them (1 Cor. 7:17–24). Yet here, Paul speaks of calling to describe what already is the case, not what we desire or what one day might be.

But is it really a problem to use "calling" in a way the New Testament does not? Not necessarily. As long as both speaker and listener know what is happening, one can use a biblical word in a sense that, while not strictly biblical, is not unbiblical either. Something like this is the case with systematic theology's use of the word "regeneration" to mean "new birth." But the test of all specialized theological terms, whether drawn from Scripture or not, is how well they map the biblical territory they refer to. "Trinity," for instance, is hard to improve. Yet I would suggest that the term "calling" is a poor guide to the biblical terrain of aspiring to vocational eldership. "Calling" attributes to God something that you cannot be sure of until it happens. "Calling" implies you know God has done something before he has done it.

And so the exegetical problem leads to another potential problem: namely, entitlement. If God has called you to pastor, who can tell you he hasn't? If God has called you to pastor, then it's high time some church out there catches up with what God is doing. I once heard a fellow seminary student ruefully reflect, "Lately, I've been questioning my calling." That makes self-examination sound like deserting your post. But what if he was asking the right questions, and the answers came back negative? It is all too easy for a sense of calling to shield its possessor from needed criticism.

Of course, it is possible to use calling language and avoid entitlement. As I mentioned above, many wise, level-headed Christians have used this language throughout the centuries without apparent catastrophe.[4] Those who wield the language most wisely distinguish between an "internal call" and an "external call." By "internal call," they typically mean an intense desire to serve as a pastor. By "external call," they tend to mean recognition and confirmation by a church. This recognition might initially take the form of encouragement from individual members, or informal support from a church's eldership, but it remains incomplete until a church calls you to be their pastor.

I do not disagree with anything that people use these terms to refer to, but I think the terms themselves are more trouble than they're worth. The phrase "internal call" sets up a subjective test for which I cannot find criteria in Scripture. How strong a desire is strong enough? Regarding the "external call," what exactly counts, shy of a church's call to serve as pastor? If one sweet, elderly sister encourages me about a sermon I preached, should I quit my job the next day? Even in its cautious, two-part form, the language of calling is like a misaligned drivetrain: you must constantly correct it in order to drive straight.

---

4   For a classic example, see Edmund P. Clowney, *Called to the Ministry* (Phillipsburg, NJ: P&R, 1964).

One point that could support using calling language, especially that of internal call, is that it aptly names many people's experience. Many men who go on to become pastors experience an overwhelming desire for the work. Typically, the internal call is identified with just such a consuming desire. Some say, "Unless you are gripped by an unrelenting, irresistible desire to become a pastor, don't do it." Charles Spurgeon put the point like this:

> The first sign of the heavenly calling is *an intense, all-absorbing desire for the work*. In order to a true call to the ministry there must be an irresistible, overwhelming craving and raging thirst for telling others what God has done to our own souls. . . . "Do not enter the ministry *if you can help it*," was the deeply sage advice of a divine to one who sought his judgment. If any student in this room could be content to be a newspaper editor, or a grocer, or a farmer, or a doctor, or a lawyer, or a senator, or a king, in the name of heaven and earth let him go his way; he is not the man in whom dwells the Spirit of God in its fulness, for a man so filled with God would utterly weary of any pursuit but that for which his inmost soul pants.[5]

To be sure, desire for the work is a biblical requirement for eldership. Paul lays down qualifications for one who "aspires to the office of overseer" and thereby "desires a noble task" (1 Tim. 3:1), and Peter says an elder must serve "not under compulsion, but

5 Charles Spurgeon, *Lectures to My Students: Complete and Unabridged* (Grand Rapids, MI: Zondervan, 1954), 26–27 (emphasis original). My rejoinder to Spurgeon is indebted to Kevin DeYoung, "A Quibble with Spurgeon," The Gospel Coalition, September 2, 2010, https://www.thegospelcoalition.org/blogs/kevin-deyoung/a-quibble-with-spurgeon/.

willingly" (1 Pet. 5:2). Further, pastoring is taxing. Pastoring drops you into a surging rapid of emotional and spiritual hazards. A man should become a pastor only if he has a sober, informed eagerness for the work. Yet I think Spurgeon goes too far. Scripture nowhere says that a pastor must not be able to be content doing anything else. And some faithful pastors are prone to discouragement. They sometimes feel they would be more content doing anything other than pastoral ministry! As one dear friend of mine recently said, "If someone offered me a job as a gardener, and it paid enough to support my family, I'd take it." He is still pastoring, and I don't think he's wrong to be.

Beyond that, Spurgeon's quote seems to imply that pastors are necessarily more filled with the Spirit than a doctor or lawyer or senator could be. But this stands in tension with Paul's insistence that the Spirit gives whatever gifts he wants to whomever he wants (1 Cor. 12:4–7, 11, 27–30). Pastors do not occupy the top rung on a ladder of Spirit-filled-ness. The body needs every member, and each needs all the others (1 Cor. 12:12–26).

So, even the "internal call plus external call" has its pitfalls. It can set up a too-subjective standard to which aspiring or current pastors must measure up, or else. Personally, I recommend ditching the language altogether. But my goal in all this is not to be a language cop. I am far more concerned about the posture than the phrasing.

Advantages of Aspiring

Speaking of posture, we will conclude the chapter by exploring five advantages of using an aspiration framework over a calling one. In my view, saying "I aspire" is more biblical, more humble, more accurate, more fruitful, and more freeing.

First, aspiring to be a pastor is more biblical. Paul opens up this category for us in 1 Timothy 3:1. This aspiration becomes even more biblical when we recognize that the office is elder, all elders are pastors, and one can do the work of a pastor without being paid for it. Capitol Hill Baptist Church, which I serve as an associate pastor, currently has twenty-eight elders. Twenty-two of those men are non-staff elders; they are not paid to pastor. And yet, on top of working long hours and leading growing families, they tirelessly teach and counsel and care for the members of our church. Sometimes I feel like some of our non-staff elders do more pastoring in their free time than I do full-time!

For biblical precedents for being "called" by God to ministry, people sometimes point to the example of prophets like Jeremiah. Didn't Jeremiah say, "If I say, 'I will not mention him, / or speak any more in his name,' / there is in my heart as it were a burning fire / shut up in my bones, / and I am weary with holding it in, / and I cannot" (Jer. 20:9). Jeremiah did indeed say that, but that is not how he became a prophet. Instead: "Now the word of the LORD came to me, saying, 'Before I formed you in the womb I knew you, and before you were born I consecrated you; I appointed you a prophet to the nations'" (Jer. 1:4–5). Jeremiah did not become a prophet by getting fire in his bones; he became a prophet when God audibly summoned him to the task.

And what about Paul? Wasn't he called to be an apostle (Rom. 1:1)? Yes, he was, by the voice of the risen Christ when he appeared to him personally (Acts 26:16). God authorized prophets and apostles in a unique manner for unique offices. None of us occupies those offices today. God used extraordinary means to call men to extraordinary offices.

Second, aspiration is more humble. Again, I do not mean that those who speak of calling are necessarily proud, or those who say "aspire" are necessarily humble. But I think that calling language tilts the playing field toward pride. Calling makes a claim and puts the burden on someone else to disprove it; aspiration acknowledges you are not there yet.

Third, aspiration is more accurate. Maybe you will become a pastor, maybe you won't. Calling calls the election before all precincts have reported. Calling implies a private knowledge of God's will and ways. If you sense a calling to ministry, how can someone else verify or falsify that claim? If that claim is ever falsified, what does it say about the calling?

Fourth, aspiration is more fruitful. Calling directs your view inward, to your own desire. Aspiration directs your view outward, to the objective requirements of the office of elder. Aspiration directs your attention to the godliness and gifts you need to cultivate if you want to serve the church in this way. If you have just an inkling of a desire for pastoral ministry, the question you should be asking is not, Am I called? or How do I know whether I'm called? but, How can I grow into the kind of man who is able to serve as an elder, and even able to serve in that role full-time?

Fifth and finally, aspiration is more freeing. Saying "I aspire" shifts your focus from the subjective to the objective. You need not struggle to discern whether you have been struck by lightning from heaven. Instead, ask: Are you qualified to elder? How pastorally gifted are you? And who besides you says so? Saying "I aspire" relieves pressure and leaves freedom in its place. Your task is not to privately ascertain God's will and then wait for others to catch up. Instead, strive for growth in godliness, and cultivate the gifts God has given you. Saying "I aspire" is freeing because it reminds you that, as always, the result is up to God.

Calling asks you to picture yourself at the end of the trail. Aspiration points out the path and tells you to take a step.

2

Aspire Humbly

For by the grace given to me I say to everyone among
you not to think of himself more highly than he ought to
think, but to think with sober judgment, each according
to the measure of faith that God has assigned.

ROMANS 12:3

IS IT PROUD TO ASPIRE TO AUTHORITY? One close friend of mine in college thought so.

We knew each other well. He was one of the first people I talked to about my growing desire to be a pastor, and he suspected my motives. His problem with my aspiration was not personal so much as categorical. Isn't it self-serving to want to be in charge? Isn't it proud to set yourself up as an example? If power corrupts, isn't it corrupt to want power?

The pastorate is an authoritative office. The New Testament tells Christians to "obey your leaders and submit to them" (Heb. 13:17). So, the answer to my friend's qualms is not to deny that there is any power in pastoring. Instead, we must begin by distinguishing godly authority from ungodly authority.[1]

---

1 For a concise, richly insightful application of a Christian concept of authority, see Andy Crouch, *Strong and Weak: Embracing a Life of Love, Risk, and True Flourishing* (Downers Grove, IL: InterVarsity Press, 2016).

Ungodly authority sacrifices others to serve self; godly authority sacrifices self to serve others. Ungodly authority lays burdens on others that the one in authority is unwilling to bear; godly authority shoulders others' burdens and equips them to carry more weight over time. Godly authority authors life and wholeness. (For all this, see 2 Sam. 23:1–4; Ezek. 34:1–24; Matt. 23:4; Mark 10:35–45; Gal. 6:2; Eph. 4:11–12.) As theologian Kevin Vanhoozer puts it, "The primary purpose of authority is to provide persons with what is needed to help others to flourish."[2]

It is not necessarily proud to aspire to pastor. Still, pride crouches at the door. Pride will pervert every good desire for godly authority that it can get its hands on. So, as you aspire to pastor, aspire humbly. Assemble a humility feedback loop. The materials are all free, and you can build it in the safety of your home. Crucial components include meditation on God's word, prayer, taking initiative to serve others, getting close enough to others for them to see your faults, and listening when they serve you by pointing out those faults.

Invite criticism. And when criticism comes uninvited, hear it, pray about it, search for all the truth you can find in it, and then act on it. "Better is open rebuke / than hidden love. / Faithful are the wounds of a friend; / profuse are the kisses of an enemy" (Prov. 27:5–6).

As we considered in the previous chapter, one form that pride can take in someone aspiring to ministry is entitlement. If you are like me, at some point in your education, one of your teachers had a sign on the wall above their desk that read, "A failure to plan on your part does not constitute an emergency on my part." All aspirants to pastoral

---

2   Kevin J. Vanhoozer, *Biblical Authority after Babel: Retrieving the Solas in the Spirit of Mere Protestant Christianity* (Grand Rapids, MI: Brazos, 2016), 87.

ministry should heed a parallel warning: A sense of calling on your part does not create an obligation to hire you on any church's part. Do not assume that anyone will ever pay you to pastor. Purify your aspiration of any trace of entitlement.

Fruitful preaching ministries tend to produce aspiring preachers. That is natural and healthy. My aspiration to pastor was kindled in such a ministry. Before I heard John MacArthur and the other pastors at Grace Community Church preach, I didn't know preaching like that existed. Then discovery birthed desire. But when the desire to pastor is born in a place of obvious blessing, it is easy to desire the results as much as the work. A packed building; a bustling congregation; a broad reach. That desire for similar fruit can harden into expectation or even entitlement.

Would you still want to pastor if your lifelong charge was twenty souls in a forgotten town? Would you still crave the work if no one ever called you "pastor" or paid you to do it?

Your desire to pastor may be consuming, but whether you will pastor is uncertain. That tension may be unsettling, but it should also be freeing. The outcome is not finally in your hands. You do not need a crystal ball that can prophecy your pastoral future. Instead, walk the tightrope of pursuing your aspiration while knowing it may not come to fruition. How can you do that? It takes wisdom.

3

Seek Wisdom

The beginning of wisdom is this: Get wisdom,
and whatever you get, get insight.

PROVERBS 4:7

IF A CHURCH EVER CALLS YOU to be their pastor, your decision to accept will have effects that ricochet into eternity. If you teach and live faithfully, God will use your ministry as a means of salvation (1 Tim. 4:16). And on the last day, you will give an account for all those saints who called you to be their pastor, and whoever came into the fold under your watch (Heb. 13:17).

If you want to someday be in a position to make that decision, you need to start making a string of wise decisions. It should go without saying that wisdom is a prerequisite to being a pastor. "Him we proclaim, warning everyone and teaching everyone with all wisdom, that we may present everyone mature in Christ" (Col. 1:28). But I am also saying that wisdom is crucial equipment for the whole process of preparing to pastor.

This chapter will have three parts. First, we will consider why wisdom is necessary on the path to being a pastor. Second, I will encourage you to seek counsel all along the path. Third, I will offer a grid for making wise vocational decisions.

Get Wisdom

What is wisdom? Wisdom is practical know-how that combines the fear of God with the knowledge of God, his commands, yourself and others, and how the world works. Wisdom is the skill of living with the grain of creation.[1] Consider:

The fear of the LORD is the beginning of knowledge;
fools despise wisdom and instruction (Prov. 1:7)

The fear of the LORD is the beginning of wisdom,
and the knowledge of the Holy One is insight. (Prov. 9:10)

Whoever despises the word brings destruction on himself,
but he who reveres the commandment will be rewarded.
(Prov. 13:13)

The purpose in a man's heart is like deep water,
but a man of understanding will draw it out. (Prov. 20:5)

The prudent sees danger and hides himself,
but the simple go on and suffer for it. (Prov. 22:3)

Wisdom is crucial for the path to being a pastor because you need it both at the end and along the way. Wisdom is necessary for the end

---

1 I owe this metaphor to Bruce K. Waltke, *An Old Testament Theology: An Exegetical, Canonical, and Thematic Approach* (Grand Rapids, MI: Zondervan, 2007), 206: "When one rebels against the rules and regulations revealed by God in the Torah . . . he or she rebels against the order of creation and will suffer the consequences. Adopting a system of ethics contrary to the revealed will of the Creator cuts against the grain; it is painful and frustrating; worst of all, it is deadly."

because if you lack wisdom, you will make a lousy pastor and should never be one. Shepherds lead sheep. They need to know what sheep need, where to find it, and how to guide them there.

You can give only what you have. You can export only what you produce. You can guide someone only through terrain you know, or when you can reliably interpret and apply the map.

But you don't need wisdom only then; you need wisdom now. Sometimes pious, well-meaning Christians treat a subjective sense of divine guidance as a substitute for wisdom. It can seem more holy, more humble even, to say "God told me" or "God led me" than to say "I think this is a wise decision." Yet nowhere in Scripture does God promise to relieve us of the burden of making decisions.[2] Instead, he promises wisdom to those who ask (James 1:5).

Ask God to give you wisdom about whether and how to pursue being a pastor. Ask him for wisdom to understand what it takes to be a pastor. Ask God for wisdom to discern what gifts he has given you and how to hone them. Ask him for wisdom to know your faults and how to correct them. Ask him to fill you with wisdom so that, whether you ever pastor full-time or not, you will walk in a manner worthy of the Lord and bear fruit in every good work (Col. 1:9–10).

Seek Counsel

How can you get wisdom? One important means is seeking counsel.

> Where there is no guidance, a people falls,
>> but in an abundance of counselors there is safety. (Prov. 11:14)

---

2 For a sensible corrective to an overly subjective approach to guidance and decision-making, see Kevin DeYoung, *Just Do Something: A Liberating Approach to Finding God's Will* (Chicago, IL: Moody Publishers, 2014).

By insolence comes nothing but strife,
  but with those who take advice is wisdom. (Prov. 13:10)

Without counsel plans fail,
  but with many advisers they succeed. (Prov. 15:22)

Plans are established by counsel;
  by wise guidance wage war. (Prov. 20:18)

Seeking counsel is simple: find wise people and get them to share their wisdom with you. Especially important here are the pastors of your church. Ask them to apply their wisdom to you and your aspiration. Ask them whether they see any pastoral gifts in you, and how you can cultivate those gifts. Ask them how you can gain pastoral experience. Well ahead of any major decisions you might make, ask multiple wise, mature believers for counsel, especially pastors. And the more experience those counselors have doing what you hope to do, the more valuable their counsel is likely to be.

At no stage of aspiring to ministry is seeking counsel irrelevant. Do you have just a glimmering of desire to pastor? That's a fine thing to tell your own pastor. Are you unsure about whether to apply to a promising but risky pastoral opportunity? Lean on counselors whose wisdom you trust—the more the better. Not for nothing does Proverbs twice urge us to hear out "an abundance of counselors" (Prov. 11:14; 24:6).

Don't just ask; listen. Seeking counsel does not mean always agreeing with it. But if the counsel you receive never changes your mind or shapes a decision, I'm not sure it's counsel you're seeking. It might just be confirmation you're after, confirmation of what you already want and think.

The goal of seeking counsel is not necessarily that your counselors will tell you what to do. For one thing, they won't always agree with each other. And a good counselor is not one who will make the decision for you. The best counselors know the limits of their wisdom. As Gandalf says to Frodo, "Even the very wise cannot see all ends."[3] You could make a decision without gaining any wisdom, and you might gain wisdom without yet coming to a decision. A good counselor is one who will ask questions you have not yet asked, and identify variables you have not yet factored in. A good counselor will help you learn how to make a wise decision yourself.

Make Decisions

Back in late 2009, I was meeting regularly with Michael Lawrence to get his counsel about preparing well for pastoral ministry. At the time, Michael was an associate pastor of Capitol Hill Baptist Church, but he had just been called to serve as the senior pastor of Hinson Baptist Church in Portland, Oregon, where he has now pastored for ten years. And, though Michael had not yet moved to Portland, he was already being peppered with questions from the members and staff of his new church. On one of our walks to get coffee, we were discussing how to discern whether one should be a senior pastor. Michael quipped, "Become a senior pastor if you want to preach all the time and make all the decisions."

Now, Michael has a certain flair for pointed overstatement. He believes, as do I, in a plurality of elders, who together shepherd the church. He believes, as do I, in the value of sharing the pulpit in order to raise up other pastors and keep a church from being too dependent

---

3   J. R. R. Tolkien, *The Fellowship of the Ring: Being the First Part of the Lord of the Rings* (New York: Del Rey, 2012), 65.

on the senior pastor. Still, the man had a point. Even in a church with a plurality of elders, the pastor who bears primary responsibility for the church's preaching and public services will need to be comfortable making decision after decision after decision.

Making decisions comes with the territory of leading. Wise leaders seek counsel. Wise leaders aim for consensus and work patiently to persuade. Wise leaders know when to delay a decision. But every leader must make decisions. Every leader must make decisions that affect not just yourself but those you lead. To lead is to confront an endless volley of decisions, like hitting balls from a pitching machine that has no "off" switch.

Below, I have drawn my custom version of a grid for making vocational decisions. The basic structure consists of three variables: desire, ability, and opportunity. I can't remember where I first encountered the original three-part grid.[4] To adapt this grid to the aspiration to pastor, I have shaded in the triangle between the three points with "your local church."

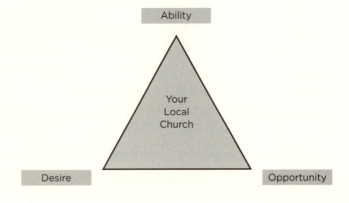

4 A brief internet search turned up its frequent use in community-based crime prevention efforts, which did not jog my memory.

This grid can help you assess your aspiration to pastoral ministry. Desire is necessary but not sufficient. And it is crucial to question the object of your desire. What about being a pastor appeals to you? How clear is your picture of a pastor's days and weeks?

Regarding ability, three crucial categories are character, content, and competence. Character: Do you meet the biblical qualifications for elders? What are your besetting sins? If everyone in your church followed your example, would the church become more holy or less? Content: How well do you know Scripture? How well can you answer doctrinal questions and dismantle errors? Are the wells of your mind deep enough for others to draw from? Competence: How well can you preach and teach God's word, counsel others from God's word, and lead people to become more conformed to Christ?

Opportunity looks different depending on what altitude you view it from. And good leaders tend to create opportunities rather than waiting for them. When you talk, do people listen? That's an opportunity to teach. Yet your ability to create or even influence opportunities has firm limits. If you apply for a pastoral opening and the church does not call you, there is nothing more for you to do there, besides praying that the church will call a godly, faithful, gifted shepherd. But on a smaller scale, what opportunities might be open to you, right now, that could help you develop gifts for ministry and better discern whether to pursue pastoring full-time?

Each of these three factors is necessary but not sufficient. Even two out of the three will not get you there. Not desire and ability without opportunity. Certainly not desire and opportunity without ability. And, though it is the most subjective, you should not pursue a ministry position that you are able to do, and have the opportunity to do, but have no desire to do. "Not under compulsion, but willingly, as God would have you" (1 Pet. 5:2).

I have shaded "your local church" into the space between all three variables, because the church of which you are a member should inform your perception of all three. You should seek counsel from your church's elders, and from other mature, trusted members, about each corner of this triangle. Counsel from within your church can foster more informed desire, a more precise assessment of your ability, and a sharper, more panoramic picture of opportunities before you. In what ways has your church affirmed your ability to pastor? What pastoral trial runs have you taken within the church, and how have other members received and responded to those?

Now, this tool has obvious limits. For one, it focuses only on you, not on those you may already be leading, like your family. What if a ministry opportunity appears that looks ideal to you, but your wife is against it? Or what if she is willing to follow you only out of a bare commitment to submit, with zero desire for the opportunity itself?

Treat the grid as a lower limit, not an upper one. These are not boxes to tick but sites for self-examination. Use this framework as a starting point for reflection, prayer, and seeking counsel. And far more than you seek an answer to the question of whether to be a pastor, seek wisdom. Call out for insight; raise your voice for understanding; seek it like silver and hidden treasure (Prov. 2:3–4). "Then you will understand the fear of the LORD / and find the knowledge of God" (Prov. 2:5).

4

Make the Biblical Qualifications Your Compass

Therefore an overseer must be above reproach.

1 TIMOTHY 3:2

MY FRIEND ANDREW WILSON, Teaching Pastor at King's Church in London, has an enviable way with words and a classically English eye for irony. The latter is especially evident in a cheeky blog post, "Two Sets of Search Criteria," which juxtaposes two descriptions of the ideal candidate for the office of pastor.[1] The first Andrew takes from an influential megachurch near Chicago:

> The senior pastor will lead and serve Willow Creek Community Church and all its locations so that it can become a thriving, healthy family of local churches. This man or woman will provide overall leadership and vision for the entire network of regional campuses.

---

1 Andrew Wilson, "Two Sets of Search Criteria," *Think* (blog), February 24, 2020, https://thinktheology.co.uk/blog/article/two_sets_of_search_criteria. Wilson anonymized the first list, but, pushy American that I am, I have lifted the veil.

They will ensure Willow Creek's vision and strategy is clear and understood across all locations, that the right leaders are leading and serving the campuses, and that Willow Creek is positioned for strength well into the future.

The senior pastor will have the ability to dream and cast vision for the next season of congregational life and community impact. The ideal candidate will demonstrate spiritual leadership, an authentic walk with Jesus, and a proven commitment to balancing the rhythms of work and life. He or she will be a proven "leader of leaders" who can motivate and inspire high-capacity men and women to use their gifts to further the vision.[2]

The second list was written in the late sixth century by a pastor in Rome, known to history as Gregory the Great:

He must, therefore, be the model for everyone. He must be devoted entirely to the example of good living. He must be dead to the passions of the flesh and live a spiritual life. He must have no regard for worldly prosperity and never cower in the face of adversity. He must desire the internal life only. His intentions should not be thwarted by the frailty of the body, nor repelled by the abuse of the spirit. He should not lust for the possessions of others, but give freely of his own. He should be quick to forgive through compassion, but never so far removed from righteousness as to forgive indiscriminately. He must perform no evil acts but instead deplore the evil perpetrated by

2 The source is a "Pastoral Search" page on Willow Creek Community Church's website, which previously was at https://www.willowcreek.org/en/about/elders-and -leadership/pastoral-search#profile, but was taken down after their pastoral search was completed.

others as though it was his own. In his heart, he must suffer the afflictions of others and likewise rejoice at the fortune of his neighbor, as though the good thing was happening to him. He must set such a positive example for others that he has nothing for which he should ever be ashamed. He should be such a student of how to live that he is able to water the arid hearts of his neighbors with the streams of doctrinal teaching. He should have already learned by the practice and experience of prayer that he can obtain from the Lord whatever he requests, as though it was already said to him, specifically, by the voice of experience, "When you are speaking, I will say 'Here I am.'"[3]

How do these two lists strike you? The first list fatigues me; the second scares me.

Here are another two lists of pastoral qualifications. Both are inspired by the Holy Spirit and written by the apostle Paul. Both say basically the same thing. Read each carefully. If you want to pastor, here is what God says you must be:

The saying is trustworthy: If anyone aspires to the office of overseer, he desires a noble task. Therefore an overseer must be above reproach, the husband of one wife, sober-minded, self-controlled, respectable, hospitable, able to teach, not a drunkard, not violent but gentle, not quarrelsome, not a lover of money. He must manage his own household well, with all dignity keeping his children submissive, for if someone does not know how to manage his own

---

3 My wording of this quote differs from Andrew's since I have taken it from Gregory the Great, *The Book of Pastoral Rule*, trans. George E. Demacopolous, Popular Patristics 34 (Crestwood, NY: St Vladimir's Seminary Press, 2007), 43–44. The end of the paragraph cites Isa. 58:9.

household, how will he care for God's church? He must not be a recent convert, or he may become puffed up with conceit and fall into the condemnation of the devil. Moreover, he must be well thought of by outsiders, so that he may not fall into disgrace, into a snare of the devil. (1 Tim. 3:1–7)

This is why I left you in Crete, so that you might put what remained into order, and appoint elders in every town as I directed you—if anyone is above reproach, the husband of one wife, and his children are faithful [ESV marginal note] and not open to the charge of debauchery or insubordination. For an overseer, as God's steward, must be above reproach. He must not be arrogant or quick-tempered or a drunkard or violent or greedy for gain, but hospitable, a lover of good, self-controlled, upright, holy, and disciplined. He must hold firm to the trustworthy word as taught, so that he may be able to give instruction in sound doctrine and also to rebuke those who contradict it. (Titus 1:5–9)

The rest of this chapter will consider what these qualifications say and what you should do about it.

What the Qualifications Say

As D. A. Carson has observed, these lists are remarkable for being unremarkable.[4] With only a couple exceptions, the qualifications given in these two lists are elsewhere required of all Christians.

---

4   See D. A. Carson, "Defining Elders," 9Marks, January 4, 1999, https://www.9marks
.org/article/defining-elders-2/. My exposition of both lists is indebted to Carson's
article. See especially Carson's discussion of "husband of one wife," offering arguments where I mainly assert.

Both lists start with "above reproach." This does not mean perfect; if it did, no church would have elders. Instead, to be above reproach is to be free of obvious inconsistency, to have no glaring fault that could be easily pointed out and agreed on to the discredit of your character.

The phrase "husband of one wife" could be more literally rendered "one-woman man." I don't think this means an elder must be married. Nor does it necessarily prohibit a divorcé who has remarried. Instead, it is best to see the qualification as requiring sexual fidelity. A married man must be faithful to his wife; a single man must be chaste and embody exemplary self-control.

Many of the other qualifications root in self-control and other fruits of the Spirit ("sober-minded, self-controlled, respectable . . . not a drunkard, not violent but gentle, not quarrelsome, not a lover of money;" cf. Gal. 5:22–23). To be "hospitable" is to offer generous help to Christians in need, especially when that need is incurred for the cause of the gospel. Hospitality is being largehearted and open-handed with whatever resources God has given you, whether time or food or home.

Two qualifications warn of being ensnared by the devil. One is that an elder must not be a recent convert, so that he does not become inflated with pride. A man must endure a few spiritual winters before being promoted to pastor. And a man must have a good reputation with nonbelievers. The trap Paul highlights here is hypocrisy. If a man is consistently godly, even nonbelievers will recognize his integrity. But if he is one man at church and another at work, he has no business being an elder. A good question to ask of any prospective elder is, Would anyone in your workplace be surprised to learn that you were a leader in your church?

The next qualification we need to consider takes a bit more work. In 1 Timothy 3:4–5, Paul writes, "He must manage his own household well, with all dignity keeping his children submissive, for if someone does not know how to manage his own household, how will he care for God's church?" Similarly in Titus 1:6, "and his children are faithful [ESV marginal note] and not open to the charge of debauchery or insubordination." Two questions confront us from Paul's teaching about a prospective elder's children: Is having children a prerequisite to being an elder, and must an elder's children be believers?

First, does this passage require a prospective elder to have children? I don't think so. Instead, I think the passage assumes what will most often be the case, rather than enacting a rule with no exceptions. In 1 Corinthians 7:32–35, Paul extols the state of singleness for its potential to secure one's undivided devotion to the Lord. Paul himself was apparently single when he wrote those words, since he referred to the other apostles as married, and not himself (1 Cor. 9:5). While Paul, as an apostle, did not hold the local church office of elder, he held an office that was even more authoritative and consequential. It would be odd to the point of contradictory for Paul to lay down a qualification for eldership that he himself did not meet. So, instead of requiring a prospective elder to have children, I think these two passages assume that most will. And a man's record as a father reveals his fitness to elder. Which brings us to our second question.

Must a man's children be believers in order for him to serve as an elder?[5] The main text of Titus 1:6 in the ESV ("believers") would

---

5 For a useful, complementary discussion that has informed my position here, see Justin Taylor, "You Asked: Does an Unbelieving Child Disqualify an Elder?" The Gospel Coalition, November 2, 2011, https://www.thegospelcoalition.org/article/you-asked-does-an-unbelieving-child-disqualify-an-elder/.

require this conclusion, but I think the marginal text, "faithful," has it right. The translation issue here is that the Greek adjective *pistos* means "faithful," which can mean either trusting or trustworthy, either depending or dependable. Three factors weigh, to my mind conclusively, in favor of the sense of "faithful" as a reference to generally obedient, reliable behavior.

The first is a theological problem for the "believers" view: no man can ensure the regeneration of his children. Only the Spirit gives new birth (John 3:8). And nowhere does Scripture promise that if a man is qualified to pastor, God will guarantee the salvation of his children. Further, interpreting the requirement this way runs the risk of absurdity. If a man is already serving as a pastor, is each new child he fathers presumed a believer unless proven to be an unbeliever? Is there a grace period in which an apparently unbelieving eight-year-old child is not disqualifying, whereas a sixteen-year-old would be? Instead, the qualification in 1 Timothy 3:4–5 and Titus 1:6 assumes a general cause-and-effect relationship between a man's leadership in his home and the behavior of his children. Governing children is at times bewilderingly difficult, but a godly man does it to good effect. This qualification holds a man responsible for what he is responsible for, not what he isn't responsible for.

Second, regarding the disputed word in Titus 1:6 itself, it makes best sense to see the following phrase as specifying negatively what the prior word says positively. That is, an elder's children must be "faithful and not open to the charge of debauchery or insubordination." There is no "and" in the Greek. Paul simply follows the positive word with a negative phrase. The negative and the positive are not two different descriptions but two halves of one image.

Third, though many translations, including the ESV, obscure this parallel, Paul uses virtually the same Greek phrase in 1 Timothy 3:4, only with a different object. We could literally render Titus 1:6 as "having faithful children" and 1 Timothy 3:4 as "having obedient children." And just like he expands on "faithful" in Titus 1:6, in 1 Timothy 3:4, Paul expands on "obedient" by saying, literally, "with all dignity." This sharpens our dilemma, because these two qualifications are exactly parallel. It would be difficult to understand how Paul could require in 1 Timothy 3:4 that an elder's children be merely obedient, and yet require in Titus 1:6 that an elder's children be regenerate. Does "obedient" in 1 Timothy 3:4 actually mean "born again"? I don't think so. Instead, by far the simplest solution, which makes sense of each passage and both together, is that in both passages Paul requires that an elder's children obey their parents. In Titus 1:6, "faithful" describes not belief but behavior.

This in turn makes best sense of the conclusion Paul draws in 1 Timothy 3:5: "For if someone does not know how to manage his own household, how will he care for God's church?" Leadership in the home is the prime proving ground for leadership in the church. A man should be entrusted with God's flock only if he has proven faithful with the flock God has already given him. Managing a household includes financial provision, competent administration, the discipline and nurture of children, and attending to the physical, emotional, and spiritual flourishing of every member of the household. As we will discuss in chapter 18, fathering and eldering extensively overlap.

How can you pursue this qualification if you are single? Consider how you steward your money, time, relationships, and resources. If you live with others, are you a peacemaker with your family members or housemates? Do you handle all your responsibilities diligently and competently so that you have time left over to serve and support others?

Finally, Paul requires that an elder be a capable teacher of God's word. We see in 1 Timothy 3:2 that "an overseer must be . . . able to teach," and in more detail in Titus 1:9 that "he must hold firm to the trustworthy word as taught, so that he may be able to give instruction in sound doctrine and also to rebuke those who contradict it." To be an elder, you must be a teacher of Scripture. You must be able to tell God's people what God's word means and what they must do about it. You must know God's word well enough to be able to demonstrate not only what it means but also what it does not mean.

Does this mean that every elder must be able to preach, in the sense of serving up the Sunday morning sermon every week? No. While every elder must be able to teach, remember that Paul himself recognizes that some elders will devote themselves particularly to teaching (1 Tim. 5:17). Godly, qualified elders can be gifted to teach God's word to different degrees, and in different formats.

These qualifications boil down to three basic points. First, an elder must be an exemplary Christian. What should be true of all Christians must be true of him. Second, an elder must be able to lead others, and the first place we should look to find that out is his family. Third, an elder must be a capable teacher of God's word. When we put these three together, we learn that an elder's most crucial means of leading are his example and his teaching. Elders walk in the ways of Christ, instruct Christ's people in those ways, and exhort others to follow. A faithful elder doesn't say, "Go ahead!" nearly as often as he says, "Come on!"

What You Should Do about It

So what should you do about these qualifications? Make them your compass.

Who even uses a compass these days? Besides Boy Scouts and backpackers, I'm not sure. You probably don't even own a compass—except perhaps in a smartphone app. So what does a compass do? It orients you. It tells you where North is, and therefore where East, South, and West are. It is then up to you to find your way. But with a compass, you always know the direction you're heading.

Everyone wants to be strategic. Politicians, entrepreneurs, pastors. A tactical player sees only the next move; strategy reads the board. Yet these biblical qualifications for eldership seem to call for a singularly un-strategic response: the plodding pursuit of character. How strategic does it seem to be sober-minded, self-controlled, or respectable? But there's nothing more strategic than the right compass bearing.

Along your path to being a pastor, you may wade into swamps of tough circumstances.[6] You may stumble through deserts of frustrated desire. You may confront chasms that seem certain to halt your progress. But in all this, the biblical qualifications for eldership tell you which way to head. No matter who recognizes you or doesn't, no matter how many teaching opportunities you get or how few, no matter which job offer you get or don't, if you are growing in these qualifications, you are growing into a pastor. Whatever seeming detours God sends you on, make progress in godliness your prime directive.

6 This paragraph borrows imagery from a discussion of moral compass bearings as strategic equipment in the "leadership lessons from history" book than which none greater can be conceived: John Lewis Gaddis, *On Grand Strategy* (New York: Penguin, 2018), 16–17.

Pursue godliness. Pursue godliness more than you pursue position or publicity or prestige. Pursue godliness more than you pursue the pulpit. Pursue godliness more than you pursue others' recognition of your godliness. Pursue godliness when no one is looking and no one cares. Pursue godliness when it seems like godliness is not getting you where you want to go.

How can you make these qualifications your compass? Memorize them. Meditate on them. Pray through them. Ask God to show you where you do not yet measure up. Make a list of the qualifications, and then come up with something you can do to grow in each of them. Consider "not quarrelsome." Do your contributions to social media consistently pass that test? What about "not quick-tempered"? When was the last time you used the excuse of "I'm just competitive" to justify an angry outburst at someone on the opposing flag football team? Or consider hospitality. What resources do you have that you could spend more generously for others? How could you open your home to provide for others' needs and seek their spiritual good?

Ask others who know you well how they would grade you on the scale of these qualifications. Seek out men who are serving as elders, especially of your own church. Ask them what they did and do to conform their lives to this biblical rule. And follow their example.

Making the biblical qualifications your compass puts pressure on your character, where it belongs, and takes pressure off your circumstances, where it doesn't. What do you care more about, repentance or recognition? If the latter, stay away from the pulpit. If you are not godly out of the spotlight, you will never be godly in it.

You cannot guarantee that a church will call you as their pastor. You might not have the opportunity to go to seminary. You may not be getting the preaching opportunities you want. Even if you are, your other responsibilities at work and at home might leave you little leisure for study and teaching. It might seem like no matter what you try, your desire to serve the Lord in full-time ministry keeps getting swatted. I do not want to downplay the frustrations or discouragement that might come with those struggles. Still, do not let any of those setbacks monopolize your attention. Instead, keep checking your compass.

PART 2

———————

WALKING THE PATH

5

Learn to Pastor from Faithful Pastors and Healthy Churches

What you have learned and received and
heard and seen in me—practice these things,
and the God of peace will be with you.

PHILIPPIANS 4:9

"NOT ENOUGH IS STUDIED ABOUT how the body keeps well. Medicine treats symptoms and doesn't get at causes. Studying disease is a backward way to do medicine. When you treat an ulcer, you're not treating what caused it. Teaching such things to a patient should be ninety percent of the practice of medicine. It's not—as done by most people." So said family practice physician Sue Cochran, as reported by John McPhee in his 1986 book *Heirs of General Practice*.[1]

How does the church body keep well? What causes a church to flourish or collapse? Do you know how to tell the difference, spiritually speaking, between symptoms and causes?

---

1   John McPhee, *Heirs of General Practice* (New York: Farrar, Straus and Giroux, 1984), 81.

Sometimes a man's desire to pastor is stoked by experiencing a lack of health in a church. That is one way that God brings good from evil (Gen. 50:20). But, as in medicine, studying negative symptoms affords only a partial, unbalanced education. If all you know about what a church should be is, "Not like that one," slow down. Reaction breeds overreaction.

A healthy church is a mature, self-healing organism. The ultimate cause of its health is always God's grace. You cannot create a healthy church any more than you can create a healthy human. But God works through means, through secondary causes. The preached word, made effective by his sovereign Spirit, is the principal instrument through which God grants a church life and health. And God works through a host of other means that apply and extend that preached word.

The best way to learn the art of pastoral medicine is by closely observing a healthy church body. Learn to pastor from faithful pastors and healthy churches. If you desire to pastor but are not, and have never been, a member of a healthy church, I would strongly urge you to join a thriving, mature church. Learn health from the healthy before you try to lead the unhealthy to health.

Think of marinating in a healthy church as akin to a medical residency. Physicians learn to practice medicine not just from books and lectures, but from a residency in which they watch experienced doctors work, and those experienced doctors watch them work. My church's pastoral internship is one version of such a residency. Observation is half the work we assign the interns. They attend every public service of the church, every elders' meeting, every pastoral staff meeting, every Sunday night service review. They sit in on membership interviews and have meals with a long list of elders, staff, deacons, and church members. They each are mentored throughout the semester by one of our pastoral staff. In all this, the goal is for them to connect the dots between biblical principles and pastoral practice. The goal is for them to see what health looks like and learn something about how to foster that health.

If you are unable to participate in a formal residency like ours, consider how you can cobble together an informal one. Ask your pastor what you might be able to observe of the church's inner workings, and on which of his pastoral rounds you might be able to ride along.

Every pastor is a sheep before he is a shepherd. One of the best ways you can prepare to pastor is by joining a healthy church and devoting yourself to being a faithful member. Whether or not a church offers you any formal training, a healthy church will incubate an aspiring pastor far better than an unhealthy one.

I have placed this chapter at the head of the path. Why? Because nearly everything I am about to exhort you to do will be helped by being a member of a healthy church and hindered if you are not. A healthy church is a greenhouse that will accelerate the growth of all the fruits I will challenge you to cultivate. Want to grow as a leader, teacher, and preacher? Stick yourself under the ministry of godly, gifted men. Do you want to start setting a godly example? Then seek godly examples. Where will you find them? In a healthy church. Want to learn the work of an elder? Then learn it from men who are doing it. Praying with breadth and depth, overcoming lust, learning to be a faithful husband and father, studying God's designs for the church, being sanctified through trials—a healthy local church will help you with all this and more. So find one, join one, and then pour your life into it.

6

Start Setting an Example

Not domineering over those in your charge,
but being examples to the flock.

1 PETER 5:3

THE DAY YOU START SERVING as a pastor is the day everyone starts watching you. Members of your church will search your face for cues, especially when something awkward happens. They will notice where you sit and who you sit with. They will comment when you get a haircut or new shoes. If part of your shirt comes untucked during a service, they might discover that before you do. To be a pastor is to be watched.

What are people looking for? That depends on the person and the occasion. What many of them are—and all of them should be—looking for is an example. The impulse to follow a pastor's example can be unhealthy, as when a pastor exceeds his mandate and abuses his authority by turning his preferences into laws. The impulse to follow a pastor's example can be gently amusing, as when members of his church, and especially young men who aspire to pastor, start to wear what he wears and talk like he talks. No pastor's personal preferences should rule others' lives. And a man's quirks of dress and speech usually matter little. But a pastor's moral example means everything.

One of the many ways modern Western culture tries to deny reality is by treating the idea of following another's example as inherently limiting, stifling, and oppressive. But opposing imitation is both blind and foolish. Imitation is inescapable. Everyone imitates. We do what our friends do. We do what people we want to be like do. As Jason Hood observes, "Few of us try sushi, social media or facial hairstyles unless we are introduced to them by a flesh-and-blood model. Humans do not learn to speak, read, write, tie shoes or perform a vocation without steady doses of imitation."[1]

Imitation has its advantages. To learn how to fix a leaking sink, would you rather read a fifty-page manual or watch an experienced plumber do the job? To paraphrase Seneca, the way of precept is long, but the way of example is short and helpful.[2]

Whose example do you follow? Who should follow yours?

Imitating others is not just a matter of habit and common-sense wisdom; it is baked into Christianity. Christian discipleship works by both instruction and imitation. As Jesus said to his disciples on the

---

1 Jason B. Hood, *Imitating God in Christ: Recapturing a Biblical Pattern* (Downers Grove, IL: InterVarsity Press, 2013), 190. Hood's work is a rich and wise treatment of Scripture's theology of imitation. See especially chapter 12 on the church as a community of imitation.

2 See Seneca, *Ad Lucilium* 6.4, in *Seneca IV: Ad Lucilium Epistulae Morales I; Books I–LXV*, trans. R. M. Gummere, Loeb Classical Library (Cambridge, MA: Harvard University Press, 1917), 27, 29: "You must go to the scene of action, first, because men put more faith in their eyes than in their ears, and second, because the way is long if one follows precepts, but short and helpful, if one follows patterns. Cleanthes could not have been the express image of Zeno, if he had merely heard his lectures; he shared in his life, saw into his hidden purposes, and watched him to see whether he lived according to his own rules."

night before his death, "If I then, your Lord and Teacher, have washed your feet, you also ought to wash one another's feet. For I have given you an example, that you also should do just as I have done to you" (John 13:14–15). Jesus makes his own love not only the motive and means but also the measure of how we must love each other: "A new commandment I give to you, that you love one another: just as I have loved you, you also are to love one another" (John 13:34; cf. 15:12). And Peter tells us that even Jesus's death, with all its unrepeatable redemptive effect, is also our example: "But if when you do good and suffer for it you endure, this is a gracious thing in the sight of God. For to this you have been called, because Christ also suffered for you, leaving you an example, so that you might follow in his steps" (1 Pet. 2:20–21; cf. Phil. 2:5–11; Eph. 5:2, 25, 28).

We are to follow not just Jesus's example but also that of other believers. "Brothers, join in imitating me, and keep your eyes on those who walk according to the example you have in us" (Phil. 3:17). Here Paul exhorts us to follow not just him but also others who follow him. Does this put mere mortals on too high a pedestal? Not at all: "Be imitators of me, as I am of Christ" (1 Cor. 11:1). Godly examples point beyond themselves to Christ. When you see a godly example, do not merely look at them—look through them.

Scripture charges pastors to lead by example, and members to follow their example. As Peter urges, "So I exhort the elders among you, as a fellow elder and a witness of the sufferings of Christ, as well as a partaker in the glory that is going to be revealed: shepherd the flock of God that is among you, exercising oversight, not under compulsion, but willingly, as God would have you; not for shameful gain, but eagerly; not domineering over those in your charge, but being examples to the flock" (1 Pet. 5:1–3). And the author of Hebrews writes to the whole assembly, "Remember your leaders, those who spoke to you the word of God. Consider the outcome of their way of life, and imitate their faith" (Heb. 13:7).

If you want to be a pastor, start setting an example. Live a life that others should imitate. Live a life that others may safely and profitably imitate. I hope you already pass your decisions and habits through the filter of what God says is good. "Finally, brothers, whatever is true, whatever is honorable, whatever is just, whatever is pure, whatever is lovely, whatever is commendable, if there is any excellence, if there is anything worthy of praise, think about these things" (Phil. 4:8). It's time to add a second filter: Does this set a good example? Could I commend this practice to others? "What you have learned and received and heard and seen in me—practice these things, and the God of peace will be with you" (Phil. 4:9). Will the God of peace be with others if they practice what you practice? Would other members of your church grow in godliness if they did what you do?

If everyone in your church studied Scripture the way you do, would they know God better and obey him more? If everyone in your church prayed the way you do, would their prayer life be richer or poorer than it is now? And your example is not limited to obviously spiritual matters. Your example includes everything you click and watch. It includes how you give and spend your money. It includes what you do to relax and unwind. It includes every word you say. It includes how you treat every person you ever meet.

Certainly, Christians' consciences are calibrated differently.[3] Setting an example does not mean never doing anything that any Christian

---

3   See the exegetically insightful, pastorally useful work of Andrew David Naselli and J. D. Crowley, *Conscience: What It Is, How to Train It, and Loving Those Who Differ* (Wheaton, IL: Crossway, 2016).

anywhere would disagree with. But it does mean taking extra care. It means caring more about someone else's holiness than about your freedom. It means always being ready to answer the question, "Well, what do *you* do?" If you need to make a significant decision, and one option leaves you in a moral gray area, setting a godly example may well mean choosing the safer option.

To be a pastor is to live your life in public. Even when you're off, you're on. If you want to be a pastor, get ready to be watched, and start setting an example worth watching.

7

Elder before You Elder

And we urge you, brothers, admonish the idle, encourage
the fainthearted, help the weak, be patient with them all.

1 THESSALONIANS 5:14

AIM TO BE MISTAKEN FOR an elder before you are appointed an elder. All pastors are elders, and every elder is a pastor. For some elders, pastoring is their job. But not all. And much confusion and harm results from treating pastoring like any other job. Hence John Piper's famous line, "Brothers, we are not professionals."[1] Even when pastoring is a job, it differs radically from every other job.

So let's work with the broader category, the office of elder. You do not apply to be an elder, get hired, and only then start to do the work. Instead, a church appoints elders. Though the term is not explicitly used in Scripture, I think it is helpful to say that a church "recognizes" elders. No individual or church can make a man an elder. Sure, a church can appoint whoever it wants to the office, but if a man does not fulfill the biblical qualifications, if a man does not desire and do

---

1   John Piper, *Brothers, We Are Not Professionals: A Plea to Pastors for Radical Ministry*, updated and expanded ed. (Nashville, TN: B&H, 2013).

the work of an elder, then whatever you call him, he is not an elder. A man is an elder only if his character and spiritual labor say so.

Which means that every elder is an elder before he is an elder. Every legitimate elder shows himself qualified in character and competence before being appointed to the office. In the previous two chapters, we examined the character half of the equation; this chapter considers competence.

The fundamental work of every elder is bringing the Bible to bear on Christians' lives and the life of the whole church. An elder leads by exemplifying obedience to God's word, teaching God's word, applying God's word to the struggles and sins of individuals, and, together with the other elders, directing the church's overall work and mission in accord with God's word. Exemplify, teach, counsel, lead. Only the last is restricted to the formal exercise of the office. You cannot lead the church as a whole unless the church asks you to. But you don't need anyone's permission to set a godly example and to teach and counsel God's word. In fact, Scripture teaches that all Christians should set godly examples, teach each other, and counsel one another.

Paul commends the whole church in Thessalonica for imitating the apostles and the Lord himself by receiving the gospel "in much affliction, with the joy of the Holy Spirit." With what result? They "became an example to all the believers in Macedonia and in Achaia" (1 Thess. 1:6–7). In doing this, the Thessalonians themselves "became imitators of the churches of God in Christ Jesus that are in Judea" (1 Thess. 2:14). And Peter exhorts us to resist Satan and stand firm in faith, "knowing that the same kinds of suffering are being experienced by your brotherhood throughout the world" (1 Pet. 5:9). So, as we considered in the previous chapter, elder before you elder by setting a godly example now. As you do, you are doing what all Christians should be, which is precisely the point of being an elder.

But Scripture also expects all Christians to teach and counsel each other. Paul, writing to all the Christians in Rome, says, "I myself am satisfied about you, my brothers, that you yourselves are full of goodness, filled with all knowledge and able to instruct one another" (Rom. 15:14). And to the church in Colossae: "Let the word of Christ dwell in you richly, teaching and admonishing one another in all wisdom, singing psalms and hymns and spiritual songs, with thankfulness in your hearts to God" (Col. 3:16). Finally, Paul exhorts the church in Thessalonica, "And we urge you, brothers, admonish the idle, encourage the fainthearted, help the weak, be patient with them all" (1 Thess. 5:14). All these passages exhort all Christians. Every Christian should teach and counsel other Christians.

So what are you waiting for? You can start now. Here are four ways to begin.

First, disciple. Discipling is simply helping others follow Jesus.[2] Deliberately do spiritual good to others to help them grow in conformity to Christ. Ask other members of your church spiritual questions, and patiently explore their answers. Pray with others. Read Scripture with others. Find another believer who seems eager to grow and regularly read Scripture together. You could meet once a week and take turns teaching each other a chapter of Romans. Discipling is speaking truth in love (Eph. 4:15). Discipling is sharing with someone else not only the gospel but also your own self (1 Thess. 2:8). Discipling can be formal or informal, regular or irregular. You

---

2   This sentence and the next echo Mark Dever, *Discipling: How to Help Others Follow Jesus* (Wheaton, IL: Crossway, 2016), 13.

can meet at the same table of the same coffee shop at the same time every week. Or you can bring someone along when you go grocery shopping, asking them questions about their walk with Christ on the way there and back.

Second, extend hospitality. Most scriptural exhortations to hospitality require material support for Christians with whom you have no prior relationship. For instance, "Do not neglect to show hospitality to strangers, for thereby some have entertained angels unawares" (Heb. 13:2; cf. Rom. 12:13; 3 John 5–8). But 1 Peter 4:9 makes hospitality a mutual obligation: "Show hospitality to one another without grumbling." So how can you provide practical help to other Christians with a view to the glory of Christ and their growth in Christ? For instance, Jeremy Mueller, a single brother who recently interned in our church, would regularly make a dinner to bring to other church members. From the other side, many families in our church will not just ask a member to babysit their kids, but will invite them to have dinner with their family before they go out, to get to know them and encourage them.

What needs can you meet? How can you make your home a hub for service and fellowship? How can you help others spiritually while serving them physically?

Some men concede to a minivan when the abundance of their children constrains them. Me, I started with one. My first car was a silver 1996 Mercury Villager that my parents generously let me take to college in Los Angeles. That minivan uncannily resembled its current successor, a silver 2011 Honda Odyssey. But during my undergraduate days, in addition to hauling surfboards and musical instruments and camping gear, my Villager was also the unofficial bus ministry from the University of Southern California (USC) campus to

Grace Community Church. Students needed rides, and the Villager had seats. Church, twenty minutes away, started at eight thirty in the morning. To park and find a seat we had to be there by eight. So, for a couple years, just about every Sunday morning, I rose by six, and got in the car by seven, to start making my rounds. Responses to the inevitable phone calls from dorm parking lots were predictable and uniform, as if scripted. "*[Muffled by pillow:]* Oh, what? Already? I'll be right down."

Third, do evangelism. As Paul charged Timothy, "Do the work of an evangelist" (2 Tim. 4:5). As Mack Stiles puts it, "Evangelism is teaching the gospel with the aim to persuade."[3] And while an elder's ministry of the word primarily aims at the members of his congregation, every elder, especially a full-time preaching pastor, should set an example of personal evangelism. Consider starting an evangelistic Bible study with non-Christian classmates or coworkers. Pray for opportunities to evangelize and make opportunities to evangelize.

Fourth, counsel. Learn to care for souls. Consider again 1 Thessalonians 5:14: "And we urge you, brothers, admonish the idle, encourage the fainthearted, help the weak, be patient with them all." What are the causes and symptoms of idleness? What words can strengthen the fainthearted? Can you help the weak, or does your eager zeal tend to trample them? Learn to diagnose diverse spiritual ailments, and to dispense the precisely tailored prescriptions that stock the shelves of God's word. Take spiritual initiative toward a wide range of Christians: young and old, eager and indifferent. Learn how to do spiritual good to people who are less and less like you.

---

3 J. Mack Stiles, *Evangelism: How the Whole Church Speaks of Jesus* (Wheaton, IL: Crossway, 2014), 26.

Every Christian has a certain spiritual profile. A person's personality, culture, upbringing, family, season of life, material circumstances, vocations and responsibilities, hopes and fears, sins and struggles, physical and emotional suffering, spiritual gifts, and spiritual maturity—all this shapes what they bring to God's word and what they get from God's word. All this informs what they need to hear and whether they are willing to hear it. The saints' gifts and graces are wildly diverse, as are Satan's devices for snaring them.[4] So learn not just to speak truth, but to speak it in love. Learn to find the lock that fits the key. Learn to serve struggling sheep not just the truth, but the right truth, at the right time, with the right tone. Be as ambitious to listen well as you are to speak well. Spurgeon once observed, "A man who is to do much with men must love them, and feel at home with them."[5] So make yourself at home among many sorts of sheep. Learn to love the saints in all their almost fantastic variety.[6] Elder before you elder.

---

4 For a penetrating guidebook on the latter, see Thomas Brooks, *Precious Remedies Against Satan's Devices* (Edinburgh: Banner of Truth, 1968).

5 Charles Spurgeon, *Lectures to My Students: Complete and Unabridged* (Grand Rapids, MI: Zondervan, 1954), 169.

6 I borrow the last phrase from C. S. Lewis's essay "Membership," in *Fern-seed and Elephants: And Other Essays on Christianity* (London: Fount Paperbacks, 1975), 18: "The sacrifice of selfish privacy which is daily demanded of us is daily repaid a hundredfold in the true growth of personality which the life of the Body encourages. Those who are members of one another become as diverse as the hand and the ear. That is why the worldlings are so monotonously alike compared with the almost fantastic variety of the saints. Obedience is the road to freedom, humility the road to pleasure, unity the road to personality."

8

Want to Be a Leader?
Then Lead Something

*He must manage his own household well, with
all dignity keeping his children submissive, for if
someone does not know how to manage his own
household, how will he care for God's church?*

1 TIMOTHY 3:4–5

PART OF WHAT IT MEANS TO elder before you elder is to lead
something else before you lead the church. Want to be a leader? Then
lead something. If you can, start with a family.

Now, as we saw in chapter 4, 1 Timothy 3:4–5 does not lay down
an inviolable rule that every elder must be married and have children.
And church history is studded with examples of stellar unmarried
pastors. Richard Sibbes, Charles Simeon, and John Stott were all lifelong bachelors. Robert Murray M'Cheyne was single, though he was
engaged to be married when he died at twenty-nine. My own church
has had single elders who are excellent, exemplary shepherds.

Still, there are reasons why Paul points to family leadership as an
entrance exam for church leadership. Like a church, a family is a

close-knit organism. Like a church, a family is populated by sinners. Like a church, a family has work to do. That work includes not just the physical but also the spiritual nurture of children (Eph. 6:4). And a husband's care for his wife, like an elder's for his flock, aims at her growth in likeness to Christ (Eph. 5:25–27).

So here is a test: Can you persuade a worthy woman to marry you? Would it be in a godly, mature Christian woman's best interest to submit to you for the rest of her life (Eph. 5:22)?

And if you do marry, eagerly embrace the gift of children. Children are a blessing from God in their own right (Ps. 127:3–5), and raising children will prod your character and your capacity to lead in ways that little else will. Being a father has done far more to prepare me to pastor than seminary ever could. Consider Herman Bavinck's lyrical celebration of how children change their parents:

> For children are the glory of marriage, the treasure of parents, the wealth of family life. They develop within their parents an entire cluster of virtues, such as paternal love and maternal affection, devotion and self-denial, care for the future, involvement in society, the art of nurturing. With their parents, children place restraints upon ambition, reconcile the contrasts, soften the differences, bring their souls ever closer together, provide them with a common interest that lies outside of them, and open their eyes and hearts to their surroundings and for their posterity. As with living mirrors they show their parents their own virtues and faults, force them to reform themselves, mitigating their criticisms, and teaching them how hard it is to govern a person. The family exerts a reforming power upon the parents. Who would recognize in the sensible, dutiful father the carefree youth of yesterday, and who would ever

have imagined that the lighthearted girl would later be changed by her child into a mother who renders the greatest sacrifices with joyful acquiescence? The family transforms ambition into service, miserliness into munificence, the weak into strong, cowards into heroes, coarse fathers into mild lambs, tenderhearted mothers into ferocious lionesses.[1]

Authority flows to those who take responsibility.[2] For what are you responsible? For what else can you take responsibility? If you are a college student, how about leading your campus ministry? If you work full-time, give yourself diligently to every aspect of your job. Work with all your might, the whole time you are on the clock (Eccles. 9:10; Col. 3:23). When you hit a snag and need to consult your supervisor, don't just report the problem, propose a solution. And in church, can you lead a small group? Or start by serving as the backup host and teacher? What about informally gathering a few men together, setting a time, and seriously studying Scripture each week?

Want to be a leader? Then lead something. Not just "someone": the "thing" part is more important than you might think. Like a company, a campus ministry, a family, and even a pick-up basketball game, a church is an institution. At bottom, an institution is a shared rule structure that shapes behavior. As Jonathan Leeman has put it, "Institutions tell you how to act, and they give you opportunities to act. They help to define relationships, giving them purpose and direction.

---

1 Herman Bavinck, *The Christian Family*, trans. Nelson D. Kloosterman (Grand Rapids, MI: Christian's Library Press, 2012), 96–97.
2 Douglas Wilson, *Father Hunger: Why God Calls Men to Love and Lead Their Families* (Nashville, TN: Thomas Nelson, 2012), 42.

They even shape aspects of your identity."[3] Many institutions share family resemblances. Leading any institution, even one as informal as a church small group, will help you lead another. Countless institutions confront the same questions. Who sets the agenda? Who makes decisions, and how? How are disagreement and dissent handled? Who appoints leaders, and on what basis? What compromises can you live with?

If you want to pastor, learn to think and act institutionally. How patient a persuader are you? How comfortable are you with the push and pull, often wear and tear, of group decision-making? How well do you earn and steward others' trust? Have you ever started an institution, even something as small as a book club or small group, and then successfully handed it off? Have you ever applied my dad's rule for campsites by leaving an institution better than you found it?

The pastoral shades into the political. Pastors need to know how much capital they have with others and when to spend it. Some men who aspire to ministry know everything about where a church should be and nothing about how to help them get there. What good is it to know the destination if you don't know where someone is starting from? What good is it to give someone directions if they don't have the gas in their tank to get there?

If you want to be a leader, start leading. Volunteer for responsibility and you will accrue authority. Learn the art of meeting people where they are and helping them take one confident step toward where they should be.

---

3 Jonathan Leeman, *Political Church: The Local Assembly as Embassy of Christ's Rule*, Studies in Christian Doctrine and Scripture (Downers Grove, IL: InterVarsity Press, 2016), 108. My discussion in this paragraph is indebted as well to page 107. Further, two paragraphs down, the phrase "The pastoral shades into the political" comes from a conversation with Jonathan many years ago.

9

Master and Be Mastered
by Scripture

I have more understanding than all my teachers,
for your testimonies are my meditation.

PSALM 119:99

SOME OF MY FAVORITE SEMINARY classes were the electives I
took with the learned, insightful, near-legendary Dr. Peter Gentry,
including Hebrew exegesis of Isaiah. The set text was Isaiah 1–11
and 54–56. We were required to read the Hebrew text of all those
chapters, using grammars and lexica as our only aids. The final exam
consisted of several portions of those chapters, chosen by Dr. Gentry
and hidden from us until the day of revelation, when the secrets of
our hearts were judged. In that exam, we had to read and translate
the selected portions, and answer questions about word formation,
verb forms, and sentence structure. Our only help on the exam was
a set of definitions for words used less than five times in all of Isaiah.

To prepare for the exam, I spent hours pacing back and forth in
empty classrooms on the Southern Baptist Theological Seminary's
campus, reading the Hebrew text aloud to myself. I would read along

with an audio recording and then read it alone. Some of the phrases still roll off my tongue eight years later. You could approach that test with confidence only if you had immersed yourself in the length and depth and breadth of all the assigned chapters of Isaiah. The only way to pass the test was to master the text.

Nearly every day that you serve as a pastor will test your ability to interpret and apply Scripture. Church members will ask you about the thorniest ethical quandaries in the Pentateuch. They will entrust to you their most intimate, complex struggles. You will need to recall, on short notice, passages that can shine light through narrow gaps into dark places of the soul. And on the last day, God will judge your work by whether you built with the precious materials he has given you in his word (1 Cor. 3:10–15). The only way to pass both the daily exams and the final exam is to master and be mastered by Scripture.

How can you master Scripture? Know Scripture deeply and broadly. Aim to grow constantly in your grasp of Scripture's depth and breadth. For breadth, I would strongly encourage you to read regularly through the whole Bible, at least once a year, for several years. The M'Cheyne reading plan is a great way to do that, and there are countless others. "All Scripture is breathed out by God and profitable for teaching, for reproof, for correction, and for training in righteousness, that the man of God may be complete, equipped for every good work" (2 Tim. 3:16–17). How can you equip people from all of Scripture if you don't know all of Scripture? How can you know all of Scripture if you don't read all of Scripture?

I was a freshman in college the first time I finished reading through the whole Bible. To my shame, I remember thinking, "Now what?" Thankfully, it quickly dawned on me that those wells had plenty more water to draw out, and always will.

Another way to pursue breadth in reading Scripture is to read through whole books in a single sitting. Read Isaiah like you would read a novel. Lock into its rhythm and flow. I guarantee it will be an edifying two hours.

What about depth? Here crucial habits are repetition, meditation, and memorization. I have profited from John MacArthur's advice about how to master a book of the Bible. Take a decent-sized book, like the Gospel of John, which has 21 chapters. Break the book into thirds and read a third every day for a month. So in January, that's John 1–7, then February is John 8–14, and March is John 15–21. In three months, you will have read the whole book thirty times. Try it. See how deep under your skin the book gets with that many repetitions. See how much of it you memorize without even trying.

Meditation is the art of patiently pressing the truth into your mind and heart.[1] Meditation is thought aimed at the heart. Meditation is savoring the truth until it flavors your soul. When you make bread or pasta by hand, as my wife and my kids and I often do, you have to knead the dough. Kneading changes the chemical structure of the mixture. Kneading forms gluten strands, which give bread its texture. Meditation is spiritual kneading. Meditation is working the truths of Scripture into your soul until they alter the structure of your heart, creating new strands of faith, hope, and love.

I would also strongly encourage you to memorize Scripture.[2] Verses are good, chapters better, and whole books best of all. If you memorize

---

1 For a wealth of practical counsel on how to meditate on Scripture, see Donald S. Whitney, *Spiritual Disciplines for the Christian Life*, enlarged and rev. ed. (Colorado Springs, CO: NavPress, 2014), 46–69.

2 For some motivation to memorize Scripture and instruction on how to do it, see Whitney, *Spiritual Disciplines for the Christian Life*, 39–45. Further, while I have not

a passage, the sheer repetition required virtually guarantees that you will also meditate on it. And memorizing puts Scripture on the tip of your tongue like nothing else does. For more than fifteen years now, I have found memorizing Scripture—especially whole books—to be an exceedingly profitable spiritual discipline. And its benefits for pastoral ministry have been immediate, lasting, and wide-ranging.

If you have never memorized a whole book before, I would encourage you to pick something short and sweet, like Philippians or 1 Thessalonians. Set a time that you will work on it each day. If you can, get a partner—like a believer you are discipling—who will memorize it with you. That way you can hold each other accountable and recite the text to each other. And, in my experience, a helpful way to memorize an extended passage of Scripture goes something like this. Start with the first verse. Say the whole thing out loud while looking closely at the words. (If the verse is long, then say the first sentence or section.) Repeat a few times. Then, without looking at the words, say the whole verse out loud. If you can do this successfully, do it five or ten more times. There. You have memorized the verse. You have it word-perfect, and now you need to keep it that way. So, the next day, start by reviewing, out loud, without looking, what you memorized the day before. If some is already rusty, brush the rust off by repeating a briefer version of yesterday's work. Then repeat the acquisition process with the next verse. Each day, repeat everything you have learned so far, and then grab the next verse. The kicker, of course, is that the more you memorize, the more time you need to spend

---

followed his method exactly, Andrew Davis, "An Approach to Extended Memorization of Scripture," is a helpful guide. Available at http://www.fbcdurham.org/wp-content/uploads/2015/07/Scripture-Memory-Booklet-for-Publication-Website-Layout.pdf, accessed April 27, 2020.

reviewing. But you can get creative. Review while washing dishes or folding laundry or sitting in traffic.

Allowing for a few missed days and a few when reviewing takes all your time, if you stick to it, you will memorize Philippians in four months. But if you want to retain what you have memorized, you need to regularly review the whole thing. It is especially important to review the book right after you have learned it. My track record on this has been mixed. I would recommend reviewing the whole book every day for at least a month. The good news is, once you know it well, you can say it a lot faster. If you want to master Scripture, memorizing it will force you to dwell on every word, and it will cause every word to dwell in you (Col. 3:16).

But the real test of whether you are mastering Scripture is whether it is mastering you. The point of studying Scripture is to submit to Scripture. The point of reading Scripture is to be read by Scripture. The point of meditating on Scripture is to be remade by Scripture. So, turn reading into praying. Turn study into self-examination. Whenever you study Scripture, keep your eyes peeled for reasons to praise God and humble yourself. Use Scripture as a searchlight to expose sins in your heart that you have not yet reckoned with. As John Webster said, the canon of Scripture is "a knife at the church's heart."[3]

Every pastor must have a thorough, firsthand mastery of the whole of sacred Scripture. And every pastor must be thoroughly

---

3   John Webster, "The Dogmatic Location of the Canon," in *Word and Church: Essays in Church Dogmatics*, Cornerstone Series (London: Bloomsbury T&T Clark, 2016), 46: "If the canon is a function of God's communicative fellowship with an unruly church, if it is part of the history of judgment and mercy, then it cannot simply be a stabilizing factor, a legitimating authority. Rather, as the place where divine speech may be heard, it is—or ought to be—a knife at the church's heart."

mastered by Scripture. Every time you attend to the words of Scripture, aim to claim more territory in your soul for the rule of King Jesus. Engage Scripture in order to surrender to Scripture. Like Jacob with the angel, in all our wrestling with Scripture, the blessing is in the losing.[4]

---

4 I borrow this image from a sermon by Mike Bullmore, at the 9Marks at SBTS conference in 2013, in which he applied the metaphor to expository preaching. Available at http://media.9marks.org/audio/9marksatSBTS_1.mp3, accessed April 27, 2020.

10

Take Every Teaching Opportunity You Can Get

Practice these things, immerse yourself in
them, so that all may see your progress.

1 TIMOTHY 4:15

WHEN I STARTED TO SERIOUSLY want to be a pastor, one of the first people I told was Brian Bunnell. At the time, Brian was studying at The Master's Seminary and leading Grace Community Church's college ministry at USC, called Grace on Campus. From the beginning, Brian tended my pastoral aspiration with care and insight. We met regularly to discuss Scripture and our spiritual lives. He loaned me his copy of Spurgeon's *Lectures to My Students*, which I devoured over Christmas break my sophomore year. And Brian gave me a key piece of advice: "Take every teaching opportunity you can get."

If you want to serve as a full-time preaching pastor, there are two checkpoints you need to clear. You must be godly enough to be an elder, and you must be a good enough preacher that a church should pay you to preach. Now, the two checkpoints are not entirely separate, since every elder must be able to teach (1 Tim. 3:2; Titus 1:9). But, as we saw in chapter 1, the New Testament ties pastoral compensation to teaching: "Let the elders who rule well be considered worthy of double honor, especially those who labor in preaching and teaching. For the Scripture says, 'You shall not muzzle an ox when it treads out the grain,' and, 'The laborer deserves his wages'" (1 Tim. 5:17–18). And consider Galatians 6:6: "Let the one who is taught the word share all good things with the one who teaches."

To slightly oversimplify, the first checkpoint does not necessarily have vocational implications, but the second does. You can serve as an elder without changing jobs. But you are reading this book because you not only want to serve as an elder, you want to spend your life in that work. So fix your focus on that second checkpoint. One of the most crucial criteria for whether you should pastor full-time is how well you preach and teach God's word. All else equal, the more you teach and preach, the clearer your path will become.

What teaching opportunities can you seek or make? Can you lead a small group or teach an adult Sunday school class? What about a kids' Sunday school? There are few better tests of your preaching than whether you can hold the attention of a room full of hungry six-year-olds. Could you preach at a nursing home or homeless shelter? Can you give an evangelistic talk at a summer camp or student event? Can you preach in your current church, or the church you grew up in, or your grandma's church? If you are pursuing preaching opportunities but they just aren't coming, ask God for them and wait patiently for his answer.

Two hefty qualifiers sitting on Brian's advice are time and obligation. When you faithfully fulfill your other obligations, how much time is left over? If you are a college student, odds are you have a lot more time than you think you do, and you could use it a lot better than you think you are. But for brothers with fuller hands, the time crunch can hurt. If you have a busy job and a growing family, "free time" may be a distant memory. Making time for public teaching may prove to be a complex negotiation. So how can you persistently meditate on God's word so that, when opportunities arise, each time you've got something better to say? When you slot in teaching opportunities, how can you discipline your preparation so that, rather than suffering from your prolonged absence, your family benefits from your meditation on the word?

Especially in the early days of aspiring to pastoral ministry, teaching in any context will help you teach better in others. Skills you learn in one setting will transfer to another. Learn to exhort and encourage in nuanced, targeted ways in a small group, and your sermon application may deepen. Learn to tell simple, lively illustrations to six-year-olds, and your sermon introductions should improve. If you apply yourself, every teaching opportunity you take will teach you more about the task and more about yourself. So take every chance you can get.

11

Pinch Hit

Be ready in season and out of season.
2 TIMOTHY 4:2

THE FIRST SERMON I EVER PREACHED, I preached on fairly short notice—maybe three days. It was the summer of 2006, and I was on a couple-week mission trip in Ukraine supporting long-term workers sent out by Grace Community Church. I had told the lead missionary, who pastored a Ukranian-speaking church plant in Kiev, of my aspiration to pastor, and he invited me to preach a baptismal sermon that Sunday. They were going to baptize a new believer in a river outside the city, and a short evangelistic message usually preceded the baptism.

I chose my text, Matthew 9:9–13, which ends, "For I came not to call the righteous, but sinners." In spare moments over the next few days, I stared at the passage and scribbled notes on a lined sheet of paper. I do not remember whether I came up with an outline. The sermon was brief, only twenty minutes or so, and I talked only half the time. The other half, speaking after every sentence of mine, was my translator. I don't remember much of what I said, but I know I preached the gospel. Afterward, one of the church's elders came up, shook my hand, looked me in the eye, and said, "You should be a preacher."

The first sermon I ever preached at Capitol Hill Baptist Church, where I now serve as a pastor, I preached on much shorter notice. It was the Sunday after Thanksgiving in 2008. Shortly before nine thirty in the morning, when our Core Seminar classes began, our senior pastor, Mark Dever, summoned the six pastoral interns, of which I was one.

Mark asked, "Which of you wants to give the evening sermon tonight?"

I waited a beat, not wanting to seem too eager a beaver, but when no one quickly bit, I did. There had been a mix-up. The elder scheduled to preach was traveling; a pastoral assistant had perhaps neglected to confirm a swap; the details are hazy. But the bottom of the barrel had been reached and scraped, and what peeled off was me.

After dismissing the other interns, Mark told me the text: Hebrews 11:21, "By faith Jacob, when dying, blessed each of the sons of Joseph, bowing in worship over the head of his staff." Mark was preaching the last several chapters of Genesis that morning, and our evening service typically features a fifteen-minute devotional on a single, topically aligned verse from the opposite Testament from the morning sermon's text. Back then, our evening service started at six o'clock. So, I had eight and a half hours to prepare. But not really. The next hour was Core Seminars, and the following two and half were the morning service. After the morning service, my wife and I were set to host beloved, long-serving church members Bob and Maxine for lunch.

I said to Mark, "I guess I better cancel lunch with Bob and Maxine."

"Oh no you don't," Mark popped back. "You will not cancel on Bob and Maxine! You'll have plenty of time to prepare your message after lunch."

Plenty. Sure, Mark. We kept the lunch appointment.

Over the next hour, the teacher of the Core Seminar I attended may not have received my full attention, as I scrambled to craft an outline and sketch a few application points on the front of my bulletin. Then came the morning service, then lunch. Around three that aftrrernoon, I finally opened my laptop and started writing.

The sermon clocked in at twelve minutes rather than the usual fifteen. Probably no bad thing. During our service review later that evening, associate pastor Michael Lawrence observed that my conclusion was somewhat abrupt. In his words, "The sermon landed with a thud." Thanks, Michael. Be glad it landed at all.

A few weeks later, another pastor of our church, Deepak Reju, fell ill on a Saturday night and asked me to teach his Core Seminar the next morning. A few months after that, with advance notice for once, I was given a six-week class to co-teach.

My favorite substitute preaching story has nothing to do with me. My friend John Lee is a twenty-four-year-old pastor's kid from Los Angeles. At time of writing, he is a member of Capitol Hill Baptist Church, and he completed our pastoral internship last year. Before John came to us, he spent four deeply formative years at Bethany Baptist Church in Bellflower, California, which is pastored by another friend of mine, P. J. Tibayan. In November of 2019, Bethany Baptist hosted a "Weekender," a show-and-tell conference on church revitalization for about twenty local pastors. The night before the conference, one of P. J.'s daughters injured her back in a gymnastics class and couldn't walk. (She's fine now!) At the time, doctors were concerned about how severe her injury might prove to be, so she spent the weekend in the hospital, and P. J. spent much of the weekend there with her. At seven that Saturday evening, P. J. informed John that he couldn't preach the next morning, and he asked, "Can you?" John had some notes on Matthew 14:13–33 that he had been planning to turn into a sermon later. Now, later became sooner. On Sunday, John preached, led a question-and-answer session, assisted with the members' meeting, led another question-and-answer session, led a service review, then preached a topical message to conclude the conference.

The moral of these stories? Pinch hit. If you get on base in one at bat, you might earn a spot in the lineup.

12

Apprentice in the Craft of Preaching

Do your best to present yourself to God as one
approved, a worker who has no need to be
ashamed, rightly handling the word of truth.

2 TIMOTHY 2:15

YEARS AGO, I HEARD SOMEONE ask John MacArthur how long it took him to prepare a sermon. He answered, "My whole life!"

As crucial as weekly hours in the study are, it takes much more to make a preacher. The good news for you is that, however seldom you might preach now, you can train and cross-train for preaching, so that each time you do, you are that much better.

Like most skills, preaching is best learned by doing it. But we just spent two chapters on that. My counsel in this chapter is: apprentice in the craft of preaching. We will focus on what you can do to grow between outings in the pulpit. "Practice these things, immerse yourself in them, so that all may see your progress" (1 Tim. 4:15). Think of this chapter as a trip to the batting cages.

Many crafts used to be, and some still are, taught by apprentice-ship. To apprentice is to train under someone competent in the craft until you can do what they do. In one sense, all of Christian discipleship follows this pattern. "A disciple is not above his teacher, but everyone when he is fully trained will be like his teacher" (Luke 6:40). But our focus here is narrower. How can you apprentice as a preacher?

The simplest way is to study at the feet of a good preacher—ideally, your own pastor. Learn to do what he does. As you sit under his preaching, in addition to listening in order to be edified, convicted, and encouraged, keep a ticker running in your mind that asks, What is he doing and how does he do it? Even as you consume the finished product, consider the ingredients. Ask your pastor about how he prepares and preaches. Ask him how much he prepares and when. Ask him what steps he works through and roughly how long each takes. Ask him what he does when he hits a wall. Ask him how he practices and revises the sermon before he delivers it. Your goal is not to make either his preaching or his process into a master sheet you must copy but to gain a model you can adapt.

I remember having dinner with Chase Sears at Bistango, an Italian place near USC's campus, in 2007. The food tasted better than the name sounds. Today, Chase is the senior pastor of Oak Park Baptist Church in Jeffersonville, Indiana, and still a close friend of mine. At the time, he was studying at The Master's Seminary and leading our campus ministry. I had recently preached one of my first full-length sermons, and he offered me kind, constructive criticism. It was Chase who introduced me to the distinction between an exegetical outline and a homiletical one. My sermon had the former—a good start—but not the latter. An exegetical outline merely describes the text. It restates what the text says but does little to digest and apply it. A homiletical outline should not merely paraphrase the text but also distill it and point it at the hearer's hearts.

When I first heard rich, insightful, expositional preaching, it sounded like magic. And there is an element of unction that the Holy Spirit alone can give, and no process or formula can guarantee. Nevertheless, expositional preaching is a craft. It is a skill that can be taught and learned. How do you eat an elephant? One bite at a time. Learn to slice preaching preparation into bite-size pieces.

Note that adjective *expositional*.[1] What does that mean? An expositional sermon takes the main point of the passage, makes it the main point of the message, and applies it to the life of the church.[2] As T. H. L. Parker has said of John Calvin's preaching, "Expository preaching consists in the explanation and application of a passage of Scripture. Without explanation it is not expository; without application it is not preaching."[3] I am convinced that expositional preaching—typically progressing sequentially through whole books of the Bible—is the best regular diet for a church. All my comments on preaching flow downhill from that conviction.

One way I try to help men who aspire to pastor apprentice as preachers is by including them in my preparation process. Speaking of apprenticing, I have adapted this practice from Mark Dever. I prepare my sermons throughout the week, and I try to have my sermon outline by Wednesday afternoon. Late Wednesday afternoon, usually about four to quarter after five, I invite our pastoral interns and a handful of other young men to work on the sermon with me. Beforehand, they

---

1   For two practical guides to expositional preaching, see David Helm, *Expositional Preaching: How We Speak God's Word Today* (Wheaton, IL: Crossway, 2014), and Mark Dever and Greg Gilbert, *Preach: Theology Meets Practice* (Nashville, TN: B&H, 2012). The definition of exposition that follows is adapted from Dever and Gilbert.

2   See, for instance, "9 Marks of a Healthy Church," 9Marks, https://www.9marks.org/about/the-nine-marks/, accessed Novermber 24, 2020.

3   T. H. L. Parker, *Calvin's Preaching* (Edinburgh: T&T Clark, 1992), 79.

must prepare an exegetical outline of the sermon text, a homiletical outline, and notes on how to apply the text. Our time together starts with them asking me questions about how to interpret the text. Then we consider the exegetical and especially the homiletical outlines they have come up with. Next, I pass around mine, and I ask them to stress-test it. Can they improve my sermon outline? They often do. Finally, I ask them how they would apply the text. What does it say or imply we should believe, love, hope, and do? What does it say to Christians, non-Christians, and the local church as a whole? How does the text comfort and convict? While they talk, I take notes. Insightful comments often make the final cut.

An apprentice learns by watching the master, listening, helping, and asking questions. And an apprentice learns by doing while the master watches, helps, questions, and comments. Watch the shifts over time:

I do—you watch—we talk.

I do—you help—we talk.

You do—I help—we talk.

You do—I watch—we talk.

You do—someone else watches.[4]

Seek feedback whenever you preach and teach. And, while you can learn something valuable from anyone's response to your preaching, the most valuable feedback will come from the most experienced preachers. So humble yourself. Seek out criticism. If you preach at

---

4 This is Andrew Wilson's presentation of Dave Ferguson's "five steps of apprenticeship." See Dave Ferguson and Warren Bird, *Hero Maker: Five Essential Practices for Leaders to Multiply Leaders* (Grand Rapids, IL: Zondervan, 2018), 131–34.

another church, maybe ask your pastor or other experienced preachers to listen to the recording and help you grow.

What else can you do to apprentice as a preacher? If you can't secure the services of a living, in-person "master" preacher, make do from several substitutes. In addition to the preaching you hear on Sundays, you might consider listening to and analyzing sermon recordings from other faithful preachers. Compare and contrast the strengths and weaknesses of your half dozen favorite preachers, living or dead. What tools and habits can you glean from each? And, if your efforts to get an older preacher to apprentice you have been fruitless so far, what about gathering a few friends into a preaching cohort? Divide a book into sections and take turns preaching it to each other, then discussing the text and the sermon together.

As one element in your self-driven apprenticeship, you could prepare sermon skeletons, like I have my Wednesday crew do. You might never put flesh on those skeletons and breathe them into life. Still, your knowledge of sermon anatomy will grow as you learn to assemble bones that fit the shape of very different passages.

Finally, work at wordsmithing. Words and sentences are a preacher's most basic tools.

Attend to words; befriend them. Learn to wield them with precision and power. Notice how words smell and taste, what images and feelings they evoke. Tune your ears to their rhythm and music. The fruits of what Spurgeon commends here are amply evident in his own sermons:

> You must be masters of words; they must be your genii, your angels, your thunderbolts, or your drops of honey. Mere word-gatherers are hoarders of oyster shells, bean husks, and apple-parings; but to a man who has wide information and deep

thought, words are baskets of silver in which to serve up his apples of gold. See to it that you have a good team of words to draw the wagon of your thoughts.[5]

In addition to befriending words, savor sentences. When my oldest daughter, Rose, was six years old, I read her *The Fellowship of the Ring*, the first volume of J. R. R. Tolkien's *Lord of the Rings* trilogy. We came to the point when, after Frodo and his friends made a nuisance of themselves at the Prancing Pony in Bree, Strider revealed himself to them. With his face "softened by a sudden smile" he said, "I am Aragorn son of Arathorn; and if by life or death I can save you, I will."[6] Rose exclaimed, "That's a great sentence!" A great character too, and eventually a great king. But if you want to be a preacher, make like Rose and revel in a great sentence.

If you want to produce powerful, compelling English, then consume it. Lots of it. Learn to recognize great writing and articulate what makes it great. Read for craft. Ask of a favorite author, How does he do that? Copy striking phrases and paragraphs into a commonplace book or Evernote file, and write your own variations on them. Spurgeon again: "Beauties of language, elegancies of speech, and above all forcible sentences are to be selected, remembered, and imitated."[7]

Writing is not preaching. You could preach down heaven but wither on the page. You could ignite the page but fizzle in the pulpit. Still, the exacting discipline of setting words in order under

5 Charles Spurgeon, *Lectures to My Students: Complete and Unabridged* (Grand Rapids, MI: Zondervan, 1954), 146.

6 J. R. R. Tolkien, *The Fellowship of the Ring: Being the First Part of the Lord of the Rings* (New York: Del Rey, 2012), 194.

7 Spurgeon, *Lectures to My Students*, 146.

the clinical light of a blank page will sharpen your speech in the pulpit. Apprenticing with your pastor is training for preaching; learning to write is cross-training.[8] Just like any teaching will help your preaching, any work on wordsmithing will help you wield words well when it matters most.

---

8 Regularly reading books about how to write has massively helped my preaching. Four favorites follow: Joseph M. Williams and Joseph Bizup, *Style: Lessons in Clarity and Grace*, 12th ed. (New York: Pearson, 2016) is the best introduction I have found to writing clear, concise sentences and cogent paragraphs. My favorite overall guide to writing style is Steven Pinker, *The Sense of Style: The Thinking Person's Guide to Writing in the 21st Century* (New York: Viking, 2014). The first two thirds of the book distill the contributions of many other valuable works; the last third is a brief usage guide. Joe Moran, *First You Write a Sentence: The Elements of Reading, Writing . . . and Life* (New York: Penguin, 2019), is witty and wise, and will tune your ear to the rhythm and music of sentences. Finally, I urge you to accept Stanley Fish's invitation to join "the tribe of sentence watchers." His book, *How to Write a Sentence: And How to Read One* (New York: HarperCollins, 2011), is a delight. How could you not love a book by an arch-postmodern English professor that ends with John Bunyan's Christian fleeing destruction, fingers plugging his ears as he cries out, "Life! life! eternal life!"

13

Read for Life

When you come, bring the cloak that I left with Carpus
at Troas, also the books, and above all the parchments.

2 TIMOTHY 4:13

IN CLASSICAL RHETORIC, *copiousness* is the ability to say something about anything. Someone who is copious has stockpiled truth and beauty, and can distribute them at a moment's notice. Copiousness is the acquired state of having something to say.

How can you acquire that state? In my experience, one of the greatest helps is constant reading. In chapter 9, we considered the priority of repeatedly reading, meditating on, and memorizing Scripture. In this chapter, I want to encourage you not to let your reading stop with Scripture.

The better your intake, the better your output. To overflow, you must first fill up. You have to get your thoughts from somewhere, and there are far better sources than the few inches between your ears. You are what you read. As the eighteenth-century philosopher and theologian Johann Georg Hamann put it, "The true genius knows only his dependence and weakness and the limits of his gifts."[1]

---

1 Johann Georg Hamann, *Sämtliche Werke*, ed. Josef Nadler, 6 vols. (Vienna: Herder, 1949–57), 2:260. Cited in Oswald Bayer, "God as Author: On the Theological

Here are five trails of reading that I have found fruitful to follow. First, read books that will help you know and teach the Bible better. Read works of biblical theology, the discipline of tracing the organic progression of God's redemptive purposes from Genesis to Revelation. For something entry-level, try T. Desmond Alexander's *From Eden to the New Jerusalem*; for a thicker steak, G. K. Beale's *The Temple and the Church's Mission*. Read works of systematic theology, the discipline of articulating as a coherent whole Scripture's teaching about God and all things in relation to God. In both method and content, a model of the genre is Steven Wellum, *God the Son Incarnate*.[2]

Second, read classics—theological ones, that is. These too will help you understand the Bible better, sometimes much more than modern books. So throw open the windows of your mind to let in what C. S. Lewis called "the clean sea breeze of the centuries":

Not, of course, that there is any magic about the past. People were no cleverer then than they are now; they made as many mistakes as we. But not the *same* mistakes. They will not flatter us in the errors we are already committing; and their own errors, being now open and palpable, will not endanger us. Two heads are better than one, not because either is infallible, but because they are unlikely to go wrong in the same direc-

---

Foundations of Hamann's Authorial Poetics," trans. John R. Betz, in Lisa Marie Anderson, ed., *Hamann and the Tradition*, Topics in Historical Philosophy (Chicago, IL: Northwestern University Press, 2012), 164.

2 Full details for these three works: T. Desmond Alexander, *From Eden to the New Jerusalem: An Introduction to Biblical Theology* (Grand Rapids, MI: Kregel, 2008); G. K. Beale, *The Temple and the Church's Mission: A Biblical Theology of the Dwelling Place of God*, New Studies in Biblical Theology 17 (Downers Grove, IL: InterVarsity Press, 2004); Steven J. Wellum, *God the Son Incarnate: The Doctrine of Christ*, Foundations of Evangelical Theology (Wheaton, IL: Crossway, 2016).

tion. To be sure, the books of the future would be just as good a corrective as the books of the past, but unfortunately we cannot get at them.[3]

A short list to start with, in chronological order: Irenaeus, *On the Apostolic Preaching*; Athanasius, *On the Incarnation*; Cyril of Alexandria, *On the Unity of Christ*; Augustine's *Confessions*; Martin Luther, *The Bondage of the Will*; John Calvin's *Institutes of the Christian Religion*; and John Bunyan's *Pilgrim's Progress*.[4]

Third, to reiterate from the previous chapter, read for craft. There are three kinds of preachers: hard to listen to, easy to listen to, and hard to ignore. Like the best preachers, the best writers are hard to tune out. They compel your eyes to stick to the page. My favorite living writer is John McPhee, reigning heavyweight champion of making anything interesting. Don't believe me? Try his book on oranges, or the United States Merchant Marine.[5]

---

3 C. S. Lewis, "Introduction," in Athanasius, *On the Incarnation: The Treatise* De Incarnatione Verbi Dei, trans. and ed. by a religious of C.S.M.V., Popular Patristics 3 (orig. pub. 1944; Crestwood, NY: St Vladimir's Seminary Press, 1977), 5 (emphasis original).

4 For capable translations and widely accessible editions in addition to that of Athanasius, *On the Incarnation*, cited above, see Irenaeus of Lyons, *On the Apostolic Preaching*, trans. John Behr, Popular Patristics 17 (Crestwood, NY: St Vladimir's Seminary Press, 1997); Augustine, *The Confessions*, trans. Maria Boulding, The Works of Saint Augustine I/1 (2nd ed.; Hyde Park, NY: New City Press, 2012); Cyril of Alexandria, *On the Unity of Christ*, trans. John Anthony McGuckin, Popular Patristics 13 (Crestwood, NY: St Vladimir's Seminary Press, 1995); Martin Luther, *The Bondage of the Will*, trans. J. I. Packer and O. R. Johnston (Grand Rapids, MI: Baker, 1957); John Calvin, *Institutes of the Christian Religion*, trans. Ford Lewis Battles, ed. John T. McNeill, The Library of Christian Classics, 2 vols. (Louisville, KY: Westminster John Knox, 1960); John Bunyan, *The Pilgrim's Progress* (Edinburgh: Banner of Truth, 1977).

5 John McPhee, *Oranges* (New York: Farrar, Straus and Giroux, 1967); John McPhee, *Looking for a Ship* (New York: Farrar, Straus and Giroux, 1990).

To read for craft is to read in order to absorb and adapt. What makes P. G. Wodehouse's metaphors ricochet off the page? What makes C. S. Lewis's illustrations so arresting and intuitive? (Hint: simple and familiar.) When you read for craft, slow down. Feel the rhythm of sentences. How do they begin and end? Savor the flavors of especially tasty phrases. Unearth the rhetorical devices that the author has carefully hidden beneath the smooth surface of the prose. What figures of speech have they used? What sentence structures and wordplays? Then copy the phrases or sentences, and write your own, using the same tools.

Fourth, read those who preach from the page. That does not necessarily mean published sermons, which are often bleached and drained in their migration from pulpit to page. Instead, I mean you should read pastors and theologians who write like the best preachers preach. The best preaching and teaching melds precise exposition, lucid illustration, and searching application. If you read writers who combine all three, not only will your mind and soul benefit, but you will learn something about how to do what they do. Two long-term favorites of mine, who have helped me even more since I became a pastor, are the Puritan Thomas Watson and the nineteenth-century Baptist pastor Charles Spurgeon. You could start with Watson's *A Body of Divinity* and Spurgeon's *Morning and Evening*.[6]

Fifth, read at whim.[7] Read what you want; read what you like. Alan Jacobs observes, "It seems to me that it is not so hard to absorb, and

---

6 Thomas Watson, *A Body of Divinity* (orig. pub. 1692; repr., Edinburgh: Banner of Truth, 1958); C. H. Spurgeon, *Morning and Evening* (orig. pub. 1865; repr., Fearn, Ross-Shire, UK: Christian Heritage, 2014).

7 This is the theme of Alan Jacobs, *The Pleasures of Reading in an Age of Distraction* (Oxford: Oxford University Press, 2011). The quote that follows is from page 17.

early in life, the idea that reading is so good for you, so loaded with vitamin-rich, high fiber information and understanding, that it can't possibly be pleasurable—that to read for the joy of it is fundamentally inappropriate." Instead, Jacobs counsels reading what gives you joy. The more you read what you like, the more you will read, and the more you will like what you read. That pleasurable cycle can fertilize a preacher's mind.

A good book is the best insurance policy against wasted time. Bring a book with you whenever you leave the house and any unexpected delay becomes a bonus. You can snatch even the smallest scraps of time for reading: a line at the bank, a wait at the dentist, ten minutes on hold with the internet company. To use well different quantities and qualities of reading time, I find it helpful to read several books at once, of varying difficulty and density.

Write in your books, and then write down the best of whatever you read. After just about every book I finish, I flip through the whole thing and write down quotes I marked and comments I made. Copying and filing choice quotes is like stashing meat in a chest freezer. When the recipe calls for it, you know what you have and where to find it.

14

Give Yourself to Prayer

In return for my love they accuse me,
but I give myself to prayer.

PSALM 109:4

I STRUGGLED WITH HOW TO begin this chapter. Then it dawned on me: pray for help. In this case, as in many others, to ask was to receive the answer.

Too often, Christians follow the pattern I just fell into. You try first, and if you fail, you pray. Instead, in all the work we do, all the appointments we keep and tasks we complete, our regular rhythm should be to pray before, during, and after. Pray before, for wisdom and skill. As much as possible, pray during, for help and strength. And pray after, for fruit and for God to be glorified.

If you aspire to pastor, give yourself to prayer. As Paul instructs us, "Rejoice always, pray without ceasing, give thanks in all circumstances; for this is the will of God in Christ Jesus for you" (1 Thess. 5:16–18). Again, "Rejoice in hope, be patient in tribulation, be constant in prayer" (Rom. 12:12). And Paul practiced what he preached: "For God is my witness, whom I serve with my spirit in the gospel of his Son, that without ceasing I mention you always in my prayers" (Rom. 1:9–10; cf. Phil. 1:3–4; Col. 1:3).

Paul exhorted believers to prayer, and he constantly prayed for other believers. In doing both, he set an example for every man who would be a shepherd of God's flock. Prayer is essential to pastoring in more ways than I have space to say. Here are just three ways prayer is crucial to pastoring, which double as three reasons why you should give yourself to prayer, now.

First, pastors must labor privately in prayer. As the apostles said when practical needs threatened to swamp their proper work, "But we will devote ourselves to prayer and to the ministry of the word" (Acts 6:4). Prayer is not mere preparation for a pastor's work; prayer is a pastor's work. Here again Paul sets the pace:

> For I want you to know how great a struggle I have for you and for those at Laodicea and for all who have not seen me face to face, that their hearts may be encouraged, being knit together in love, to reach all the riches of full assurance of understanding and the knowledge of God's mystery, which is Christ. (Col. 2:1–2)

As the following phrases clarify, when Paul says "struggle," he means wrestling in prayer. Paul's co-laborer Epaphras did the same: "Epaphras, who is one of you, a servant of Christ Jesus, greets you, always struggling on your behalf in his prayers, that you may stand mature and fully assured in all the will of God" (Col. 4:12). That Christians may stand mature and fully assured in all the will of God is the goal of everything a pastor does. Prayer is a direct, indispensable means to that end.

Second, pastors must lead publicly in prayer. Too many church services are virtually void of prayer. A few sentences sent heavenward between songs, a brief petition to open the sermon: that's about it. But in our corporate gatherings, we Christians should give ourselves to prayer, and pastors should lead the effort. Mark Dever has often urged pastors, "Devote so much time to prayer in church that nominal Christians will grow bored talking to the God they only pretend to know."[1] Every time I preach, I lead our congregation in a several-minute-long intercessory pastoral prayer. That pastoral prayer is a solemn responsibility, a stirring joy, and a vital pastoral tool. Normally, that pastoral prayer comes after a prayer of praise, a prayer of confession, and a prayer of thanks, all led by different members of the church.

Third, pastors must teach credibly on prayer. John Calvin said that prayer is "the chief exercise of faith . . . by which we daily receive God's benefits."[2] Scripture is bursting with exhortations to pray and examples of prayer. To faithfully expound those Scriptures, pastors need to teach people why to pray, what to pray, and how to pray. To teach these things credibly, we must know them all by experience.

The great hazard of leading in prayer and teaching on prayer is hypocrisy. Public prayer should well up from a spring of private prayer. Teaching on prayer should be backed by private practice. Now, there is a sense in which we all preach better than we live. To faithfully declare God's standards is to convict yourself for failing to meet them. This is true of more than just prayer. Often, after I finish a two-hour session of premarital counseling in the afternoon, I come home for dinner a kinder, more attentive husband than I otherwise would have been. More than once my wife has asked me, "Did you just

---

1 See, for instance, the installation sermon available at https://www.9marks.org /message/four-ps-faithful-pastorate/, accessed May 7, 2020.

2 See the title of book 3, chapter 20 in John Calvin, *Institutes of the Christian Religion*, trans. Ford Lewis Battles, ed. John T. McNeill, The Library of Christian Classics, 2 vols. (Louisville, KY: Westminster John Knox, 1960), 2:850: "Prayer, Which Is the Chief Exercise of Faith, and by which We Daily Receive God's Benefits."

finish premarital?" But there is a difference between imperfection and hypocrisy. Integrity means striving for the standard, however imperfectly. Integrity means living in such a way that any reasonable person would see a close fit between what you say and what you do.

How can you do this now? I have four practical encouragements.

First, pray before your day gets going. Thomas Brooks counsels, "He that will attend to closet prayer without distraction or disturbance, must not, first, slip out of the world into his closet, but he must first slip into his closet before he be encompassed about with a crowd of worldly employments."[3]

Second, pray the Bible.[4] Take Scripture into your mind and heart, and send it back to God through your lips. When Scripture unveils a glimpse of God's glory, praise him for it. When Scripture's arrows of conviction find their mark in your heart, confess your sin and pray for growth. When Scripture names one of the innumerable benefits God has given you, thank him for it. When Scripture points the way to greater conformity to Christ, pray for your own and others' progress. Psalms and Proverbs are especially easy to turn into prayer—not least because the Psalms already are! Another good starting point is the apostle Paul's petitions for the congregations he wrote to (Eph. 1:15–23; 3:14–21; Phil. 1:9–11; Col. 1:9–14; 1 Thess. 3:9–13; 2 Thess. 1:11–12).[5]

Third, pray systematically for the members of your church. A membership directory with members' names and pictures is a huge help. I

3   Thomas Brooks, *The Secret Key to Heaven: The Vital Importance of Private Prayer*, Puritan Paperbacks (orig. pub. 1665; repr., Edinburgh: Banner of Truth, 2006), 189.

4   For superb, simple counsel on this, see Donald S. Whitney, *Praying the Bible* (Wheaton, IL: Crossway, 2015).

5   See D. A. Carson, *Praying with Paul: A Call to Spiritual Reformation* (Grand Rapids, MI: Baker, 2014).

keep mine in my Bible. Almost every morning, I pray through a page of it. Often, my petitions are informed by a passage of Scripture I have just been meditating on. Sometimes, I will pray through a psalm or chapter of Proverbs verse by verse.

Fourth, grow fluent in praying in each of Scripture's genres of prayer: praise, confession, thanksgiving, petition, and lament. The acronym ACTS—adoration, confession, thanksgiving, supplication—can be a helpful scaffold for private and public prayer. You can gain fluency in these different genres of prayer by meditating on a single passage of Scripture and using it as a prompt for each. Praise celebrates and honors God for who he is and what he has done for us in Christ. Confession acknowledges how you have strayed from God's ways and failed to do his will. Thanksgiving recognizes God as the giver of every good gift and glorifies him for his generosity. Thanksgiving also drives out anxiety by filling your heart with calm trust in God's provision. Supplication asks God for what we know he wants to give. And, though it has no place in the tidy acronym, lament has a prominent place in the Psalms.[6] Lament voices the pain of living in a fallen and cursed world, brings our doubts and confusion to the Lord, and confesses his goodness and faithfulness.

Are you ever frustrated because you wish you could do more ministry? You can—pray. What can prayer do? Thomas Brooks again: "Oh, the power of private prayer! It hath a kind of omnipotency in it; it takes God captive; it holds him as a prisoner; it binds the hands of the Almighty; yea, it will wring a mercy, a blessing, out of the hand of heaven itself."[7]

---

6   For a moving and instructive introduction to lament, see Mark Vroegop, *Dark Clouds, Deep Mercy: Discovering the Grace of Lament* (Wheaton, IL: Crossway, 2019).

7   Brooks, *The Secret Key to Heaven*, 35.

15

Banish Pornography

Flee from sexual immorality.

1 CORINTHIANS 6:18

DO NOT LET PORNOGRAPHY torpedo your aspiration to pastor.

Scripture exhorts all believers, "But sexual immorality and all impurity or covetousness must not even be named among you, as is proper among saints" (Eph. 5:3). And pornography does far more than name sexual immorality.

Pornography is addictive. The easy, quick hit of pleasure rewires your brain to crave more. Pornography is secretive. It deceives you into thinking that, because no one else sees your sin, God doesn't either. Pornography is corrosive. It poisons your heart and mind. As Justin Holcomb observes, "Porn teaches its consumers that women exist for the pleasure of men and that their purpose is to be degraded and dehumanized for men's excitement."[1] Pornography dulls your conscience. It makes "sin look normal and righteousness look strange."[2] Pornography

---

1   Justin Holcomb, "Porn Is Not Harmless. It's Cruel." The Gospel Coalition, October 16, 2017, https://www.thegospelcoalition.org/article/porn-is-not-harmless-its-cruel/.

2   I borrow this phrase from Kevin DeYoung, *The Hole In Our Holiness: Filling the Gap between Gospel Passion and the Pursuit of Godliness* (Wheaton, IL: Crossway, 2012), 118, though he focuses on worldliness in general.

is exploitative. It trades on the degradation of women, and it fuels demand for prostitution. In Andy Naselli's words, "Pornography is to sex slavery what gasoline is to the engines of motor vehicles."[3] For these and dozens of other reasons, flee from pornography, as you should from all sexual immorality.

Further, viewing pornography undermines your fitness for the office of elder. A man who deliberately derives pleasure from watching others commit grievous sin is a man who lacks self-control (1 Tim. 3:2; Titus 1:8). Using pornography betrays a failure to bring your sexual appetites into submission to Christ's authority. To be self-controlled is to master sinful desire; to indulge in pornography is to submit to sinful desire. Using pornography also violates Paul's charge that an elder must be a one-woman man, which calls for exclusive sexual fidelity (1 Tim. 3:2; Titus 1:6). For a single man, that means consistent chastity. Finally, a man who views pornography is not above reproach (1 Tim. 3:2; Titus 1:6). You who preach against sexual immorality, do you practice it in private?

Pornography can be the German U-boat that sinks your hope of pastoring.

My point here is not to say just where the disqualifying line is. My point is that the line exists. Which side of it are you on? Is pornography keeping you on the wrong side?

If you have been sinning sexually by viewing pornography, I have three words of counsel for you. First, confess your sin to God. "If we confess our sins, he is faithful and just to forgive us our sins and to cleanse us from all unrighteousness" (1 John 1:9).

---

3 Andrew David Naselli, "Seven Reasons You Should Not Indulge in Pornography," *Themelios* 41, no. 3 (2016): 480; available at http://tgc-documents.s3.amazonaws.com/themelios/Themelios41-3.pdf.

Second, confess your sin to others, and enlist their help. "Therefore, confess your sins to one another and pray for one another, that you may be healed. The prayer of a righteous person has great power as it is working" (James 5:16). I would especially encourage you to confess your sexual sin to a pastor or elder of your church. Ask for their help and counsel. Ask them if you can contact them when you feel vulnerable to temptation.

Third, wage a multifront war for sanctification, attending to your head, heart, habits, and hardware. Let's consider each.

Your head: When you give in to temptation, what lies are motivating or enabling that act? What aspects of God's character are you ignoring? What promises of God are you failing to trust?

Your heart: What are the sins behind the sin of pornography?[4] What forms of folly and pride are weakening your defenses against temptation? What sins of the heart are creating conditions in which lust can ripen? For instance, anxiety and stress can prompt you to crave a mindless release, and discontent leaves you vulnerable to a promise of instant pleasure.

Your habits: Each day, give yourself to prayer and meditating on God's word. And cultivating self-control in other areas of your life will help you master lust.

Your hardware: What makes pornography such a plague is easy access. So cut off every access point. Do whatever it takes to make it difficult for you to reach pornography. That could mean putting a filter and accountability software on your computer and phone. It

---

4   I owe this question, and the follow-up questions that follow, to the insightful article by John Henderson, "The Sins Behind the Sin of Pornography," *9Marks Journal*, October 30, 2018, https://www.9marks.org/article/the-sins-behind-the-sin-of-pornography/.

might mean trading in your smartphone for a "dumb" phone. Does that sound radical? It's nothing compared to cutting off your hand (Matt. 5:30). To be sure, a ten-foot wall is no match for an eleven-foot ladder. That is why I addressed your head, heart, and habits before your hardware. Your most important assignment is to put lust to death (Rom. 8:12–13; Col. 3:5–6). But Proverbs calls the man a fool who passes along the street near the corner of the adulteress (Prov. 7:7–8). Today, the street corner is in your pocket, so put up whatever roadblocks and warning signs you need.

16

Marry Wisely

An excellent wife is the crown of her husband,
but she who brings shame is like rottenness in his bones.

PROVERBS 12:4

IF YOU ARE SINGLE, what are you looking for in a wife? How is your search shaped by your desire to pastor?

"Pastor's wife" is not a biblical office. The role has no biblical qualifications or job description. Nevertheless, being married to a pastor typically exposes a woman to difficulties and demands that she would not otherwise face. Her household management, her children's behavior, her schooling choices, the food she serves, and much more are scrutinized and commented on, both to her face and behind her back. Her husband's schedule is often inconvenient and irregular. His ministry can place extra demands on the family, even at times, such as holidays, when other families can relax. She must support a husband whose work can embroil him in conflict and drain his emotional reserves. And she is never far from the pressure of other church members', especially other women's, expectations of what a pastor's wife should be and do. Pastor's wife is not an office, but it is work.

The question you want to ask is, What godly, single woman do you know who is cut out for work like this?

I do not mean to paint a dour, one-sided picture. A pastor's wife also shares in the abundant joys that come from laboring for others' eternal good. But these joys appeal only to the spiritually minded. These joys are joys only to one whose heart is calibrated to heaven.

The book of Proverbs tells you what to look for in a wife. Seek a wife who is excellent, prudent, peaceable rather than quarrelsome (Prov. 12:4; 19:14; 21:9; 25:24; 27:15). And Proverbs 31 presents a lavish portrait of such a wife. She does her husband good, works diligently, runs her household skillfully, gives generously, turns raw material into profit, laughs at the future, and teaches wisely (Prov. 31:12, 13, 14–16, 18, 20, 24, 25, 26). Now, this is an ideal picture. This woman has servants at her command and wealth at her disposal. But the point is what she does with what she has.

If you want to find a wife like this, take Proverbs 31:30 to heart: "Charm is deceitful, and beauty is vain, / but a woman who fears the Lord is to be praised." Whether written or unwritten, conscious or subconscious, just about everyone who wants to be married has a list of what they want in a husband or wife. What's on your list? Scratch off "supermodel" and see what godly woman you now start to notice.

Marry wisely. That means marrying a woman who is not only godly but also likeminded. Can a woman not just join but thrive in a church you would see as faithful and healthy? If you are a convinced credobaptist, but a woman you are interested in is committed to infant baptism, then some patient theological dialogue is in order. You need to be of one mind before you become one flesh.

My point is not that you should put a potential wife under a microscope. Especially if you and she are young, you are looking for good beginnings. Apply to her the same standard you would want her to apply to you.

And beware stereotypes. As soon as my now-wife, Kristin, and I started dating seriously, I told her that I intended to pursue pastoral ministry. Her mental picture of a pastor's wife was Martha Stewart singing a vocal solo while wearing a floral dress. She was and is none of those things—though she has always been a generous host, and she has become a magician in the kitchen. Kristin's mental picture of a pastor's wife made her anxious about becoming one. But over the years, between having friends in ministry and now doing it ourselves, we have discovered a wide diversity of faithful pastors' wives. Some work outside the home; others do not. Some publicly teach women in their church and beyond; many do not. Some are natural in the spotlight; others shun it. Some are polished queens of hospitality; others serve simple fare in less-gleaming settings. Seeing this fruitful diversity has been liberating and encouraging.

Faithful pastors' wives are not cookies to be cut. Their personalities and spiritual gifts will differ widely, but the common thread is godliness. A pastor's wife must be willing to make costly sacrifices, gladly and repeatedly, for the good of Christ's people. Marry a woman like that, and she will multiply your ministry. Mine certainly has.

17

Lay Down Your Life for Your Wife

*Husbands, love your wives, as Christ loved
the church and gave himself up for her.*

EPHESIANS 5:25

YESTERDAY, I LED A SESSION of premarital counseling with an
engaged couple. At one point, I read Ephesians 5:22–33, then asked
the woman, and then the man, what in Paul's instructions to them
seems hardest. The man's reply focused on verse 25. "Well, if it just
said 'love your wives,' that wouldn't sound too hard. It's the phrase 'as
Christ loved the church' that's the kicker."

The previous chapter focused on the sacrifices a pastor's wife must
make. But the sacrifices go both ways. Your charge as a husband is
to give yourself up for your wife. Sometimes that means sacrificing a
ministry ambition or opportunity in order to serve her. Your wife is
not a tool for you to use to advance your ministry. She is not a resource
for you to spend on pastoring. Your church can always get another
pastor; your wife can't get another husband.

In twelve years of marriage so far, the worst I have done at this was
my first year of seminary. Our first child, Rose, was born in January
of 2010. Both she and Kristin suffered grave complications in the

delivery. When we arrived in Louisville that August so I could begin studying in person at Southern, Kristin was carrying serious physical and emotional pain. It was a hard time to start over somewhere new. To support us financially, I worked as an editor for 9Marks about twenty-five to thirty hours a week. On top of that, I took a more than full-time course load: five courses in the fall, two intensives over winter break, and five more classes in the spring. Why so much? I intended to pursue a PhD after seminary and wanted to pastor after that. I wanted to finish all that schooling as quickly as I could so I could arrive at my desired destination. I was impatient.

So, that first year, in addition to spending a full workday working for 9Marks, attending lectures, and completing schoolwork, I studied most evenings. We attended church every Sunday morning and evening, and our small group, and had people over for meals regularly. My work and studies did not suffer, nor did our church involvement, but my wife did. Kristin needed more help than I was giving. She needed more help with Rose, more help with housework, and she especially needed more emotional and spiritual help. She spoke up repeatedly, asking why I needed to be so busy. But I kept hitting the override button.

A few godly friends pressed me about whether my pace was wise. But the counsel that opened my eyes came from Tom Schreiner, a professor of New Testament at Southern. We were having lunch one day at his dining room table. I don't remember how the subject of busyness arose, but I admitted that my pace was causing tension in my marriage. Tom's wife, Diane, happened to pass through the room. In his frank, guileless way, Tom asked her, "How long were we in seminary, Diane? Three years, four years? Was it five? I don't remember." Then he said to me: "In thirty years, you won't remember how long it took you to do seminary, but you will remember if your wife hated you the whole time!"

Well, that did the trick. That summer, I started working for 9Marks a little more, to provide for us more comfortably, and I cut my course load in half. I gained much more time to give to Kristin and Rose. I grew quicker to help at home. I learned to be more emotionally present. I started listening at least a little better than I had for the past year.

But I didn't just learn to be less busy; I learned to be busy better. The more diligently I served Kristin and Rose when I was with them, the more willing Kristin became to send me to the study with a blessing. Sacrificing ambition for her good meant not just saying no to work but also saying yes to her. It meant finding out what kind of help she wanted most and giving it gladly. And the more I said yes to Kristin, the more willingly she said yes to my work. After a more modest pace in years two and three, we spent a fourth year in Louisville, in which I earned a ThM. Completing a ThM in just a year, while working thirty hours a week, meant that I was nearly as busy as I had been that first year. But we did not endure anything like that first year's strain. Why? Because I had learned the hard way how to put her interests before my own. I had taken some small step toward laying down my life for her.

Sometimes, faithfulness on your wife's part will mean denying herself so you can spend yourself in ministry. Sometimes, faithfulness on your part will mean saying no to ministry so you can minister to your wife. In the past couple of years, I have declined several outside preaching and teaching requests, and even canceled an international trip, because I judged that my responsibilities at home took priority.

Laying down your life for your wife is in her best interest, your best interest, and your church's best interest. It is obviously in her best interest: your sacrifices serve her sanctification (Eph. 5:25–27).

It is in your best interest because failing to live with your wife in an understanding way will hinder your prayers (1 Pet. 3:7). And what do you think that would do to your preaching? Finally, you will serve your church best if there is harmony in your home. When you need to visit a church member who is in dire need for the second time that weekend, on top of officiating a wedding on Saturday and preaching on Sunday, it will matter for your ministry whether your wife is smiling or crying when she kisses you goodbye at the door.

Do you want to give yourself away for Christ and his people? Care for your wife in such a way that she will be just as happy to give you away as you are to be given away.

18

Pastor Your Children

Fathers, do not provoke your children to anger, but bring
them up in the discipline and instruction of the Lord.

EPHESIANS 6:4

I'VE HEARD IT SAID THAT a new father has lots of opinions and no experience, and one with grown children has lots of experience and few opinions. My oldest child is ten, so I suppose I'm halfway there. Some days it seems the only sign of accumulating experience is that my confidence about how to parent steadily drains away.

For me, in being both a pastor and a father, an unnervingly common experience is having no idea what to do. To a married couple locked in years-long trench warfare, what can I say that will not trigger a landmine? At home, a property dispute breaks out over which small human may legitimately claim this Lego figure or that half of the couch. Each makes a seemingly airtight case. Your move, Dad.

Scripture's instructions to fathers are simple, but that does not make them easy. "And these words that I command you today shall be on your heart. You shall teach them diligently to your children, and shall talk of them when you sit in your house, and when you walk by the way, and when you lie down, and when you rise" (Deut. 6:6–7).

"Fathers, do not provoke your children to anger, but bring them up in the discipline and instruction of the Lord" (Eph. 6:4). The charge is clear: disciple your kids.

Parents and pastors have the same mission, though their starting points and contexts differ. The business of both is making disciples. And one of the best ways you can prepare to pastor and grow as a pastor is by pastoring your children.

If you are married, desire to be a pastor, do not yet have children, and are actively putting off having children, you might want to rethink the logic of that position. Especially if you are putting off children *so that* you can prepare for ministry. I am not laying this down as an ironclad rule. My "might" three sentences back is genuine; exceptions exist. If you move to seminary at twenty-two years old, newly married, with a wife who is willing to support you financially for a time, it might be good stewardship to seek to delay children for that season, or part of it. If you do, watch out for the burdens that will lay on your wife. Still, in general and all things being equal, a man who is a father is more ready to pastor than a man who is not. Of course, the equation differs for couples who struggle with infertility, which is its own test of a man's ability to shepherd.

Parenting enrolls you in full-time training for your character and competence as a leader.

Before I became a father, I would not have said I have a problem with anger. Raising four children has disabused me of that illusion. I am not naturally a patient person, and I would not say that prior to having children I had made any great progress in the virtue. How patient am I now? Who knows. Not as patient as I should be. But if I now have at least a small flour-sack of patience in the pantry of my character, most of it has been ground, grain by grain, by the millstone of parenting. As for competence as a leader, being a father requires you to provide, protect, oversee, manage, mediate, reconcile, teach, train, model, explain, and correct—and that's just in the hour before bed.

Like pastoring, parenting is a weight you can never fully shrug off. Like pastoring, parenting requires you to enter into experiences that differ drastically from yours, and to bear emotional burdens that would otherwise remain remote. Like pastoring, parenting plugs you into all the high highs and low lows of lives other than your own. Parenting at once shrinks your world and vastly expands it. Children change you in ways you did not know you needed to be changed.

Like church members, children have eagle eyes for inconsistency and hypocrisy. Like church members, children are far more likely to do what you do than do what you say. As James Baldwin wrote, "Children have never been very good at listening to their elders, but they have never failed to imitate them."[1]

How can you pastor your children? Continually teach them God's word. Lead them in family devotions. Short, frequent, and flexible is better than idealistic and inconsistent. Over the years, our family's approach has steadily morphed. We started with story Bibles, memory verses, and children's catechisms. We have memorized short psalms and longer chapters of Scripture. Over the past few years, we have focused on simply reading Scripture sequentially, followed sometimes by brief discussion, and more regularly by prayer based on the passage. Sometimes, the older children and Kristin and I take turns reading and praying aloud; often, I simply lead both. If we have time, we sing a verse or two of a hymn. We have found that breakfast offers the most

---

1 James Baldwin, *Nobody Knows My Name: More Notes of a Native Son* (orig. pub. 1961; repr., Vintage: New York, 1993), 61–62.

regular window for our main time of family worship. Our kids tend to be fresher and calmer at breakfast than they are at bedtime. For at least a few minutes while they eat, they are a captive audience. And ministry obligations virtually never pressure our breakfast window, whereas they often compress our evenings. My point is not to say you should do what we do, but simply to get your wheels turning. When it comes to family devotions, just about anything is better than nothing.

Finally, attend to your children individually. Learn their temperaments, tendencies, and typical temptations. Convert your knowledge of their strengths and weaknesses into compassion. "As a father shows compassion to his children, so the LORD shows compassion to those who fear him. For he knows our frame; he remembers that we are dust" (Ps. 103:13–14). Learn to adapt your counsel to their constitutions. As much as you can, as often as you can, give each of them your undivided, delighted attention. Learn to love what they love because you love them. One wise father of several grown children recently told me that, when his kids were growing up, he wanted his attitude toward each of them, and the quality of time he spent with them, to convince each of them that they were his favorite.

19

Study God's Blueprints
for the Church

*According to the grace of God given to me, like
a skilled master builder I laid a foundation,
and someone else is building upon it. Let each
one take care how he builds upon it.*

1 CORINTHIANS 3:10

MEASURE TWICE, CUT ONCE. So say carpenters and surfboard shapers. As with haircuts, you can always cut more off, but whatever you cut off you cannot put back on.

You have to know what you're building before you build it. Before you build a house, study the blueprints. So where are the blueprints for the local church? In Scripture, primarily the New Testament, especially Acts and the epistles. If you want to be a pastor, study God's blueprints for the church.

I use "blueprints" loosely. Scripture nowhere presents us with a complete, systematic equivalent of a book of church order. We have to gather a complete picture of how a local church should be ordered by comparing, collating, and drawing inferences from many passages of Scripture. To do ecclesiology well, you need well-developed systematic theology muscles. You must be comfortable with, and adept at discerning, good and necessary consequence.[1]

The first question you need to settle is, does Scripture tell us how a local church should be ordered and structured? To put it more technically, does the New Testament provide a prescriptive polity for local churches?[2] For several reasons, I would argue that it does. Though it is mere and skeletal, the New Testament does indeed present a consistent pattern of church polity. And, in the New Testament, apostolic practices function as binding precedent for all churches (cf. 1 Cor. 11:16). Further, though this would take much more work to prove, I would assert that the passages that establish the main lines of New Testament church polity carry normative force in themselves (e.g., Matt. 18:15–20; Acts 14:23; 1 Cor. 5:1–13; Titus 1:5). For these reasons and more, the issue of how to structure churches is a need Scripture meets. To put it theologically, church polity falls within the illuminating and liberating reach of the sufficiency of Scripture. As the nineteenth-century Baptist theologian William Williams put it,

---

1 See the Westminster Confession of Faith 1.6: "The whole counsel of God concerning all things necessary for his own glory, man's salvation, faith and life, is either expressly set down in Scripture, or by good and necessary consequence may be deduced from Scripture: unto which nothing at any time is to be added, whether by new revelations of the Spirit, or traditions of men." In *The Westminster Confession of Faith and Catechisms: As Adopted by the Presbyterian Church in America* (Lawrenceville, GA: Christian Education and Publications, 2005), 5. Available at https://www.pcaac.org/wp-content/uploads/2019/11/WCFScriptureProofs.pdf.

2 I address the question of whether the New Testament provides a prescriptive model of church polity at length in "Why New Testament Polity Is Prescriptive," *9Marks Journal*, July 16, 2013, https://www.9marks.org/article/journalall-churches-saints-why-new-testament-polity-prescriptive/. Throughout this chapter, I compress and repurpose arguments from that longer essay.

Should the disciples of our Lord regard this organization as a model obligatory upon them to adopt, or has he left the form of church polity discretionary with his people? . . . If any and all forms are not equally adapted to subserve the high ends for which churches are divinely instituted, then there is a form better adapted than others; and if there be one better adapted than another, the Saviour would surely not leave it to fallible human wisdom to find it out. . . . We must believe, in view of the important bearing of the form of their organization upon the successful or unsuccessful accomplishment of the high ends of their institution, that they were under the guidance of the Holy Spirit in this matter, as well as in the enunciation of the doctrinal principles of Christianity: so that the polity instituted by them must be regarded as the expression of divine wisdom on this subject.[3]

There are four overlapping aspects of the church's life and order that I would encourage you to study.[4] First, the ordinances of baptism

---

3 William Williams, *Apostolical Church Polity* (Philadelphia, PA: American Baptist Publication Society, 1874), repr. in Mark Dever, ed., *Polity: Biblical Arguments on How to Conduct Church Life* (Washingdon, DC: Nine Marks Ministries, 2001), 543–46.

4 On the topics discussed in the following paragraphs see Jonathan Leeman, "Introduction—Why Polity?" in *Baptist Foundations: Church Government for an Anti-Institutional Age*, ed. Mark Dever and Jonathan Leeman (Nashville, TN: B&H Academic, 2015), 1–23; Bobby Jamieson, *Going Public: Why Baptism Is Required for Church Membership* (Nashville, TN: B&H Academic, 2015); Bobby Jamieson, *Understanding Baptism* (Nashville, TN: B&H, 2016); Bobby Jamieson, *Understanding the Lord's Supper* (Nashville, TN: B&H, 2016); Jonathan Leeman, *Church Membership: How the World Knows Who Represents Jesus* (Wheaton, IL: Crossway, 2012); Jonathan Leeman, *Church Discipline: How the Church Protects the Name of Jesus* (Wheaton, IL: Crossway, 2012); Jonathan Leeman, *Don't Fire Your Church Members: The Case for Congregationalism* (Nashville, TN: B&H Academic, 2016); Matt Merker, *Corporate*

and the Lord's Supper. Not just their significance and proper subjects but also how they give a local church its institutional form and order.[5] Second, church membership and discipline. Who belongs to the church, and on what basis? These are the most foundational questions of polity. They define what the church is by defining who the church is.

These first two elements, the ordinances and membership, are two lenses on the same reality. What is the difference between a crowd and a church? Polity. A church is a gospel people who have formed a gospel polity. A church is a group of Christians who have committed to worship Christ together and oversee one another's discipleship. The signs of their mutual commitment are the ordinances (or sacraments), especially the Lord's Supper. Baptism binds one to many, and the Lord's Supper makes many one (see Acts 2:38–41 and 1 Cor. 10:16–17). Baptism and the Lord's Supper are the visible, public means by which God's people are marked off from the world. Baptism and the Lord's Supper draw a line around a church, and thereby draw the line between the church and the world. Baptism and the Lord's Supper turn a crowd of Christians into a church. They compact a church into a defined shape, a shape called church membership.

Once you have a church, the question naturally arises as to who has authority. How should decisions be made? Who ultimately decides who is in and out? Does the church have any recognized officers? If so, what are they required to be and do? (Hint: elders and deacons. See

---

Worship: How the Church Gathers as God's People (Wheaton, IL: Crossway, 2021). In the discussion of the ordinances above, I recycle and rephrase a few sentences from my works listed here.

5   I borrow the phrase "institutional form and order" from Oliver O'Donovan, *The Desire of the Nations: Rediscovering the Roots of Political Theology* (Cambridge: Cambridge University Press, 1996), 172. I discuss O'Donovan's point in *Going Public*, 142–43.

Phil. 1:1; 1 Tim. 3:1–13.) Here we arrive at polity proper, what most people think of when you say "church polity." So, the third element to study is the distribution and exercise of authority in a local church. Who has final authority over matters of membership and discipline? I am convinced that is the gathered congregation as a whole (see Matt. 18:17; 1 Cor. 5:4–5; 2 Cor. 2:6).

Fourth and finally, consider carefully what Scripture teaches about corporate worship. How does Scripture govern a church's gathered worship? Are we permitted to do anything not forbidden by Scripture, or are we permitted to do only what Scripture commands, exemplifies, and implies? What elements belong in a church service, and what forms fittingly facilitate those elements?

Why should you care about church polity? Why does it matter how the church should order its life together? Polity tells you who you are responsible for and who is responsible for you. It tells you who is accountable to you, and to whom you are accountable. Polity tells you how the church should make decisions, and therefore what work you need to do to lead the church to make good ones.

Pastoring a church is a profound joy, but I would never want to pastor a crowd. A crowd comes and goes at whim. A crowd is all desire and demand, no commitment. But a church is born out of mutual commitment to Christ and each other. Now *that* I can work with.

20

Serve Outside the Spotlight

The greatest among you shall be your servant.
Whoever exalts himself will be humbled, and
whoever humbles himself will be exalted.

MATTHEW 23:11–12

WHEN I WAS A MEMBER OF Third Avenue Baptist Church in Louisville, the senior pastor, Greg Gilbert, once asked during a Sunday evening service, "Who would like to preach the evening devotional sometime?" A few dozen eager male hands go up. Pregnant pause. Then, "Which of you are currently serving in the nursery or children's ministry?" Many hands drop to a low soundtrack of laughter.

Jesus's warnings to the Pharisees are harrowing reading for the aspiring pastor:

"They do all their deeds to be seen by others. For they make their phylacteries broad and their fringes long, and they love the place of honor at feasts and the best seats in the synagogues and greetings in the marketplaces and being called rabbi by others. But you are not to be called rabbi, for you have one teacher, and you are all brothers. And call no man your father on earth, for you have one Father, who is in heaven. Neither be called instructors, for you have one instructor, the Christ. The greatest among you shall be your servant. Whoever exalts himself will be humbled, and whoever humbles himself will be exalted." (Matt. 23:5–12)

The antidote to hypocrisy is humility. What good deeds do you do that are seen by few or none? When did you last volunteer for a menial task? Which title means more to you, "brother," which you are, or "pastor," which you hope to be? Is being a servant your idea of greatness?

One of the best things an aspiring pastor can do is serve outside the spotlight. Give elderly members rides to church. Serve in the nursery. Teach children's Sunday school. Volunteer to serve food at, and clean up after, the wedding reception of a couple of church members you barely know.

Everybody wants to be a servant until they get treated like one. Pastors not only are servants; they get treated like servants. Prepare yourself now for both the work and its reception by serving others. The best preparation for the spiritual trials of the spotlight is serving cheerfully in the shadows.

The church I help lead is overflowing with men who aspire to be pastors. In assessing these brothers, one question our elders regularly ask is whether a man serves in ways that do not evidently advance his ministry ambitions. What about you? If I audited the categories of your church involvement, would "something in it for you" appear in each?

Are you as eager to spend time with a lonely, introverted church member on the margins as you are to hang out with your senior pastor? An aspiration to lead can easily develop a calculating, mercenary streak. Scan your heart for signs of such subtle, cancerous pride, and operate before it can metastasize.

When the sons of Zebedee asked Jesus for glory, he promised them suffering instead: "You do not know what you are asking. Are you able to drink the cup that I drink, or to be baptized with the baptism with which I am baptized?" (Mark 10:38). Unlike rulers of the Gentiles, leaders in the church are to be not lords but servants, not striving to be first but making ourselves slaves (Mark 10:42–44). To ask one of a child's favorite questions, "Why should I?" Just keep reading: "For even the Son of Man came not to be served but to serve, and to give his life as a ransom for many" (Mark 10:45). The reason the eternal Son of God became incarnate was to serve you by giving his life for you.

I know more than one pastor who, in the early years of his ministry, not only preached every Sunday, but cleaned the church's toilets just as often. Why not clean some now?

21

If You Can, Make the Most of Seminary

Do your best to present yourself to God as one
approved, a worker who has no need to be
ashamed, rightly handling the word of truth.

2 TIMOTHY 2:15

YOU WILL HAVE NOTICED by now that most of this book is not about seminary. That is because most of preparing to pastor happens outside of seminary. I do not say that to belittle seminary education. I have two seminary degrees, and I regard that time, money, and effort as well spent.

Seminary can be a tremendous asset to your present training and future ministry. But earning a seminary degree is not a realistic possibility for every man who aspires to pastor. And, increasingly, seminary education takes many forms. The advent of the fully online MDiv has made it possible to "go to" seminary without going anywhere. My counsel in this chapter is simple: if you can, make the most of seminary.

"If you can": not everyone can or should. Not every man who aspires to pastor will have the financial means, or the time, to pursue a seminary degree. And it is not necessarily the case that everyone who can, should. I think of Blake Boylston, who once served as a bivocational pastor, then spent four years on staff at Capitol Hill Baptist Church (CHBC) as an assistant pastor, and is now the pastor of Chaffee Crossing Baptist Church in Fort Smith, Arkansas. Blake has no seminary training. He is in his mid-thirties, with three children. He is a gifted preacher, perceptive counselor, and courageous leader. He knows the Bible inside and out. Certainly, he would learn much from a seminary degree, but in his case, I doubt the gain would justify the opportunity cost.

If you are unable to pursue a seminary degree, whether soon or ever, do not view that as a disqualifying failure. Some of the best preachers I know do not have seminary degrees. Neither did John Bunyan, Charles Spurgeon, or Martyn Lloyd-Jones.

Seminary cannot make you a pastor, but it can help you become a better one. So, if you do pursue a seminary degree, how can you make the most of it?

For many, the first question is whether to study in person or online. All sorts of factors play into how you might answer that question. If you can move to a seminary with a solid faculty and study full-time, you will likely get far more out of the experience than you would by studying online. But those are big "ifs."

Money matters. How will you pay for tuition and living expenses? Will you be able to study full-time and take your pick of classes and professors, or will you have to work full-time and squeeze lectures and study time into tight margins?

Church matters too. What opportunities for pastoral training does your current church afford, and how fully are you able to take advantage of them? Further, if you do move to seminary, what church would you likely join, and how might that affect your path to pastoring? Healthy churches in seminary towns can be glutted with aspiring pastors. You might have more opportunities to teach in a month at your current church than you would in a year at a "seminary church." Then again, if your current church is doctrinally weak and crippled by division, you might learn far more from three years in a thriving, faithful church, even if you spend more time on the bench than you would like.

Depending on your circumstances and resources, either choice can prove wise and fruitful. My dear friend and fellow CHBC pastor Isaac Adams did his whole MDiv online. Why? As Isaac explained to me, "The church was loving me well, and I was growing. I saw more opportunities for growth here. And even the possibility of becoming an elder at some point." Later in Isaac's MDiv studies, CHBC did appoint him as an elder, which confirmed his decision to stay put. "That external affirmation and the prospect of pastoral experience outweighed the benefits of studying in person. If I knew I had no prospect of being an elder for another five years, I probably would have moved. And the church would have supported me either way." Isaac also had a job—doing administrative work for a Christian non-profit—that allowed some flexibility to study and gave him easy, regular access to leaders and members of the church.

What would have led Isaac to choose differently? "If I had a job that offered no flexibility to study, that would have made it harder. If I had intended to be a scholar, or a pastor-scholar, I likely would have moved to seminary. And it would have been a much different calculus if I were in a church that had few aspiring pastors and did little to train them. So much of ministry is caught rather than taught. The elders' table was its own seminary for me."

By staying at CHBC, Isaac told me, "I gained the opportunity to grow with and love one family. My trajectory was clarified by the people who knew me best. They got to deal with me." And the church offered its own version of many of the intangible benefits of being at seminary. "Because of the internship, CHBC has its own mini-seminary. Being in DC, lots of pastors and professors pass through. Some of our pastors have PhDs in theology. One of the main benefits of seminary is building a network of godly, likeminded brothers who are also aiming to pastor, and CHBC was already giving me that."

How would Isaac counsel those studying remotely? He advises:

- It's a grind. Resist the temptation to feel like you're just pushing through it. Realize this is a unique season of life, especially if you're studying while working full-time.
- If you can, start soon. It's easier to juggle work and study when you have zero kids than when you have four.
- Cultivate local dialogue partners. Talk to your pastors and others about what you're studying. And reach out to professors. Whenever you visit the campus, try to get time with them.
- Never miss church for the sake of classes. If you need to get a B on a paper to get an A in life, get the B. You've made the decision to make your location primary, so make it primary. Don't let your world shrink to the size of your computer screen.
- Set regular times to study. Get out of the house.
- Exercise. Especially given that you're not walking around a campus, it could easily be that the most walking you do is from your kitchen to your living room desk. Yes, Paul says bodily discipline is of little profit, but that does not mean no profit.

- Don't cheat. It's easier to cut corners when you're not in the classroom.
- Trust the Lord with whatever decision you make. Let your identity rest in Christ. If you study online, there's no asterisk next to your degree. What matters more than the format of your degree is what you make of it.

My own course through seminary started very similarly to Isaac's. I interned at CHBC in the fall of 2008 and started working as an editor for 9Marks in 2009. That summer, I started taking some online courses at Southern. For the same reasons as Isaac, I thought hard about staying at CHBC for several years and completing my degree online. In the end, the leading reason why I decided to move to Louisville for seminary was that I intended to pursue a PhD afterward, so I wanted to maximize my academic experience. I'm glad I did, and not just for how it set up further study. Among other factors, studying in person enabled me to build deep relationships with professors, to form lasting, fruitful friendships with fellow students, and to give some of my best hours of the day to splitting open my mind and shaking in as much Hebrew and Greek as it could hold. Studying in person enabled me to get much more out of seminary by giving more of myself to seminary.

Whether you study online or in person, how can you make the most of seminary? In one sense, almost every chapter in this book helps answer that question. But here are a few targeted tips.

First, your goal in seminary is not to fill a shelf but to dig a well. Focus on developing skills more than assimilating information. By skills, I mean thinking critically, researching patiently, and writing clearly. I also especially mean the skills of competently reading Koine Greek and biblical Hebrew.

In my view, the best benefit of seminary is the biblical and theological toolkit it helps you to amass and hone. One of the most crucial tools in that toolkit is exegesis in the original languages. My wife and I have a quick, easy way to decide what to order in a restaurant. We ask, "What are we *not* going to make at home?" Few of us have the discipline and dedication to home-cook Greek and Hebrew. The expertise of professors, structure of a formal course, and potential for public shame are all huge helps in learning ancient languages. For most students, learning the biblical languages is several orders of magnitude more difficult than learning church history or systematic theology. Send the most troops to where the battle is fiercest and the gain greatest. I would encourage you not only to fulfill the minimum requirements in Greek and Hebrew, but to do anything possible to take electives where you put the languages to work in the exegesis of biblical books.

Second, expect to be stretched. You should be stretched intellectually. You will be exposed to questions you did not know to ask, much less know the answer to. You will be exposed to textual challenges and apologetic issues that may unsettle you. You will be required to devote long hours to studying topics that seem of little immediate payoff for ministry. Stay at your post. Your job in seminary is not just to learn answers, but to learn to ask better questions, and to learn to stay on the trail long enough to find good answers. Better a good question than a bad answer.

You may also be stretched financially, emotionally, even physically. Study is long work, hard work, and often dull work. "Of making many books there is no end, and much study is a weariness of the flesh" (Eccles. 12:12). You may be stretched emotionally through uncertain circumstances, escalating responsibilities, and hopes deferred or deflated. And few families find seminary to be a financially flush season. Whatever trials God sends your way, whatever pressures he causes to compound on you, thank him for them and embrace them. If God is stretching you, then lean in, breathe deeply, hold the pose, and find the knots.

Finally, even if you are studying full-time in person, treat seminary as a supplement. Even during seminary, your local church should be the primary context and means of your pastoral training. Churches raise up pastors with supplemental help from seminaries, not vice versa. As devoted as you should be to your studies, be even more devoted to your church.

22

Improve Your Trials

Count it all joy, my brothers, when you meet
trials of various kinds, for you know that the
testing of your faith produces steadfastness.

JAMES 1:2–3

SOME PASTORS SEEM TO HAVE bottomless natural wells of sympathy. You enter their presence and instantly want to tell them the worst things you have ever done. A current of attentive, affirming kindness surfaces in every facial expression and flows through every question.

Me, not so much. My natural store of sympathy is more like a summer job's paycheck: easily spent. But the Lord has been working on me. Marrying a woman with a normal emotional range and radar has clearly helped. (Her names for me include "The Robot" and "The Machine.") So has having three daughters. But if I had to single out the one means by which God has added the most cubic inches to my well of sympathy, it would be trials. Suffering has taught me sympathy like nothing else has.

I mentioned earlier that the birth of our daughter Rose, in January of 2010, was attended with serious complications. Kristin labored through the night, and Rose should have arrived, but did not. When

Rose's heart rate became unsteady, Kristin was quickly scheduled for a C-section. In what became an emergency C-section, we learned that Kristin had suffered a placental abruption that had gone undetected throughout labor. Abruptions can be fatal for both mother and child. Doctors later told us that if the C-section had happened five minutes later, Rose would have been stillborn.

Thankfully, Rose recovered quickly. After a week in the NICU, she came home. But Kristin was not recovering. Over the course of a week, her health rapidly declined. She experienced excruciating pain. She could not move or eat. Doctors repeatedly tried and failed to diagnose what was wrong. Finally, they discovered that the problem was peritonitis, an infection of the abdominal cavity. Peritonitis is often life-threatening, and it was for Kristin. They immediately scheduled surgery, without which Kristin would have died. By God's grace, the surgery succeeded. Kristin spent another week recovering in the hospital and then she came home, still physically shattered. She could barely sit up or walk. Kristin recently had a doctor tell her that what she went through is the worst possible scenario that still has mom and baby alive at the end.

At that point Kristin had been a Christian for only three and a half years or so. When the shockwaves started settling, she said to me, "I don't feel like a baby Christian anymore." While brief, the trial was intense, and its effects linger. We were initially unsure whether it would be physically possible or medically advisable for Kristin to have more children. And physical and emotional burdens from the birth have stayed with us for years.

When Kristin was pregnant with our second daughter, Lucy, she was understandably overwhelmed with anxiety. In those months, I quickly ran out of helpful or encouraging things to say. Kristin once asked me, "Why don't you say anything when I tell you how I'm struggling?"

I replied, "Because I don't know what to say!"

"Then just say that," she said.

Inch by inch, the well expands. On the cosmic scale, the suffering I have so far endured is a very small dose. Yet even that small dose has rendered me far more able to weep with those who weep (Rom. 12:15). Even that small dose has taught me much about where to find comfort and how to give it. "Blessed be the God and Father of our Lord Jesus Christ, the Father of mercies and God of all comfort, who comforts us in all our affliction, so that we may be able to comfort those who are in any affliction, with the comfort with which we ourselves are comforted by God" (2 Cor. 1:3–4).

The New Testament is brimming with teaching about the sanctifying effects of trials:

> Not only that, but we rejoice in our sufferings, knowing that suffering produces endurance, and endurance produces character, and character produces hope, and hope does not put us to shame, because God's love has been poured into our hearts through the Holy Spirit who has been given to us. (Rom. 5:3–5)

> Count it all joy, my brothers, when you meet trials of various kinds, for you know that the testing of your faith produces steadfastness. And let steadfastness of have its full effect, that you may be perfect and complete, lacking in nothing. (James 1:2–4)

> In this you rejoice, though now for a little while, if necessary, you have been grieved by various trials, so that the tested genuineness

of your faith—more precious than gold that perishes though it is tested by fire—may be found to result in praise and glory and honor at the revelation of Jesus Christ. (1 Pet. 1:6–7)

Trials train us, but not automatically. To profit from trials, you must improve them. When God sends you suffering, keep alert to what weaknesses in your faith and character they might reveal. Learn to depend on God more desperately, to plead his promises more fervently. Suffering is a stewardship: How can you turn it to spiritual profit?

In pastoral ministry, suffering is never far away. Whatever else may vary in ministry, shepherding suffering members is a constant. And ministry will add to your share of suffering. For those future sheep's sake and your own, learn to suffer well now. God is wise to send you suffering, has wise plans for your suffering, and intends for you to grow wise through suffering. Take to heart this exhortation from Charles Spurgeon:

> Winter in the soul is by no means a comfortable season, and if it be upon thee just now it will be very painful to thee; but there is this comfort, namely, that *the Lord* makes it. He sends the sharp blasts of adversity to nip the buds of expectation: He scattereth the hoar-frost like ashes over the once verdant meadows of our joy: He casteth forth his ice like morsels freezing the streams of our delight. He does it all, He is the great Winter King, and rules in the realms of frost, and therefore thou canst not murmur. Losses, crosses, heaviness, sickness, poverty, and a thousand other ills, are of the Lord's sending, and come to us with wise design.[1]

---

1 C. H. Spurgeon, *Morning and Evening* (orig. pub. 1865; repr., Fearn, Ross-Shire, UK: Christian Heritage, 2014), 702 (emphasis original).

23

Filter

He must not be a recent convert, or he may be puffed up
with conceit and fall into the condemnation of the devil.

1 TIMOTHY 3:6

EVERY WEEKDAY MORNING, between emptying the dishwasher and starting to cook breakfast for my family, I brew two twelve-ounce cups of coffee, one for my wife and one for me. The coffee's flavor matters as much to me as its medicinal value, so each morning I grind just the beans we need, then brew the coffee by pour-over. First, you pour just enough water to soak the grinds. Let it sit thirty seconds so the carbon dioxide can off-gas. Then slowly pour in the rest of the water. It will take two or three more minutes to drip through the filter. There are far more efficient ways to brew twenty-four ounces of coffee. But those quicker methods will not produce the same depth of flavor.

In an editorial reflecting on failures in the so-called Young, Restless, and Reformed movement, D. A. Carson has written, "When rapid growth takes place, it is easy to promote people too rapidly."[1] As an

---

1   D. A. Carson, "The Underbelly of Revival? Five Reflections on Various Failures in the Young, Restless, and Reformed Movement," *Themelios* 39, no. 3 (2014): 405;

antidote, Carson invokes Gautam Mukunda's "leadership filtration theory." Here is Carson summarizing Mukunda:

> In most industries and organizations, he argues, leaders are "filtered": they are tested, scrutinized, battered a little, and they learn a great deal as they slowly rise through the system. A few leaders make it through "unfiltered," and these "extreme leaders" tend to be either geniuses or wackos. I'm not sure this analysis is always accurate, but what is obvious is that when a movement is expanding rapidly there is more opportunity for leaders to rise into positions of real power without ever having been "filtered."

My advice to you is simple: filter. Be willing to submit to processes that seem inefficient. Quicker methods will not produce the same depth of character.

How have you been filtered? How are you being filtered? How might you yet be filtered before God deems your ministry fit for public consumption?

God uses different numbers and types of filters on different men as he alone determines. Leading a family is one. Do it well and you will daily grow in your ability to lead beyond your family. Your job is another, especially if you don't like it. No man should turn to pastoral ministry as an escape pod from a job he hates. It might be that staying for a year or three in a job you don't like would do far more for your character and future ministry than quitting now.

Other filters are built into the formal and informal structures of local churches. One is simply gaining experience without title or pay.

---

available at http://tgc-documents.s3.amazonaws.com/themelios/Themelios39.3.pdf. The following quote is from the same page.

Another is the possibility of serving as an unpaid elder—a lay elder or "non-staff" elder—before you serve full-time. Obviously, becoming an elder before you are paid to be one depends on your church's needs and a host of other factors, such as how long you have been a member at your church and whether you are willing to stay there a good while longer.

Still another filter would be serving in some kind of entry-level ministry role. Our church, for instance, employs four pastoral assistants. These are young men who aspire to be pastors and have completed our internship. Usually, they either have completed seminary or study part-time while working as pastoral assistants. They tend to serve for a year or two, occasionally longer. Their job descriptions are mainly administrative, offering logistical support for public services and music, the membership process, members' meetings and elders' meetings, our pastoral internship, missionary support and missions travel, the schedule and teaching materials for adult Sunday school, coordinating counseling appointments, and so on. Pastoral assistants continually look over the pastors' shoulders. They obtain a longer, closer exposure to the daily realities and rhythms of pastoral ministry than interns who are with us for only five months. They observe elders' meetings and sit in on membership interviews and participate in service review. And, though it is not part of their job description, they tend to have regular opportunities to teach publicly.

A final filter could be serving as an associate or assistant pastor. I will say more about this in chapter 25. Serving as an associate pastor is not for everyone. Most churches can afford to pay only one pastor, if that. And associate pastor roles can have plenty of pitfalls—such as narrow, program-bounded silos and conflicts over philosophy of ministry. But, if an associate pastor role affords you the opportunity to work with a godly, likeminded pastor whom you trust implicitly, and to gain general pastoral experience as opposed to merely running programs, then consider it carefully. Serving in a supporting pastoral role might slow you down, but slowing down might be the best thing for you.

I do not list these filters as if they are a series of checkpoints you must clear. Very few aspiring pastors will pass through all of these. But here is a principle that fits them all: being under authority is a filter, as is being in authority. Different roles offer different proportions of the two. The best preparation for being in authority is being under authority. And the better you handle a little authority, the more fit you are for more. "One who is faithful in a very little is also faithful in much, and one who is dishonest in a very little is also dishonest in much" (Luke 16:10).

In all this, seek counsel. Invite your pastors to adjust your trajectory and velocity. Let your church set your pace.

How do you respond when you do not get what you want? How do you handle deferred hopes? Your response to thwarted ambitions is one of the best indexes of your maturity. A closed door can also be a filter.

What about Spurgeon? Didn't he become the pastor of a large, center-city church when he was nineteen? Yes. And the first sermon he preached as pastor of New Park Street Chapel in London's Southwark borough was his 673rd.[2] Would you call that filtered or unfiltered?

---

2   See *C. H. Spurgeon's Autobiography: Complied from His Diary, Letters, and Records, by His Wife, and His Private Secretary; Vol. I. 1834–1854* (London: Passmore and Alabaster, 1899), 321.

PART 3

APPROACHING THE DESTINATION

24

Slay and Resurrect Ambition

For where jealousy and selfish ambition exist,
there will be disorder and every vile practice.

JAMES 3:16

ARE YOU AMBITIOUS? If so, what are you ambitious for? Ambition, like faith, is only as good as its object. Unlike faith, a fountain from which other virtues flow, the wrong kind of ambition is a spring spouting vices.[1]

Pastors, and most men who aspire to be pastors, are more likely to be too ambitious than not ambitious enough. Odds are, some of your ambitions are the wrong kind. Some of your ambitions need slaying. They have the wrong object or have grown too large, so that they squash competing duties and balancing virtues. "But if you have bitter jealousy and selfish ambition in your hearts, do not boast and be false to the truth. This is not the wisdom that comes down from above, but is earthly, unspiritual, demonic. For where jealousy and

---

1 Here I echo Scott R. Swain, *The Trinity*, Short Studies in Systematic Theology (Wheaton, IL: Crossway, 2020), 90: "The faith that alone receives God and the good things offered to us by God in the gospel does not remain alone but is a principle from which other virtues spring forth."

selfish ambition exist, there will be disorder and every vile practice" (James 3:14–16).

How can you tell whether your ambitions are godly or ungodly? Here are three tests.

Godly ambition aims at God's glory; ungodly ambition aims at yours. How addicted are you to people's praise? Can encouragement cheer your heart without going to your head? Are you willing to speak hard truths if it means being passionately disliked? Are you willing to lead a church to health if health comes at the cost of size?

Godly ambition energizes you to joyfully fulfill all the duties of your many roles; ungodly ambition leads you to neglect less-glamorous duties in favor of those that glitter. Pastoral ministry is an evergreen excuse to neglect your family. The work is never finished. The needs are never all met. One of the best tests of whether your ambitions are the right size and shape is whether your wife feels like she consistently comes in second to ministry in the contest for your affections. Is your wife used to being less important to you than the church is?

Godly ambition fosters contentment with whatever obscurity or notoriety the Lord ordains; ungodly ambition creates coveting and competition. "Why does he get to pastor a church that's grown to five hundred in five years, and write books, and speak at conferences, when I'm stuck here with fifty people in a decrepit building we can't afford to repair?" Remember when, after Jesus's resurrection, Peter fell prey to something like that impulse:

> Peter turned and saw the disciple whom Jesus loved following them, the one who also had leaned back against him during the supper and had said, "Lord, who is it that is going to betray you?" When Peter saw him, he said to Jesus, "Lord, what about this man?" Jesus said

to him, "If it is my will that he remain until I come, what is that to you? You follow me!" (John 21:20–22)

Most pastors I know, myself included, need to hear this rebuke again and again: "What is that to you? You follow me!" F. D. Bruner commented on this verse, "One of the most crippling temptations in Christian work is to compare one's work with the work of an envied or admired other."[2] Can you rejoice when others succeed in ways you want to but haven't? Are you happy to do good for which you will get no credit?

Scripture commands us to put all sin to death:

For if you live according to the flesh you will die, but if by the Spirit you put to death the deeds of the body, you will live. (Rom. 8:13)

Put to death therefore what is earthly in you: sexual immorality, impurity, passion, evil desire, and covetousness, which is idolatry. (Col. 3:5)

How can you mortify selfish, ungodly ambition? Here are three ways.

First, pursue communion with Christ. Find contentment in Christ through communion with Christ. Let George Müller show you the way: "I saw more clearly than ever, that the first great and primary business to which I ought to attend every day was, to have my soul happy in the Lord."[3] The more satisfied you are in Christ, the less you

---

2   Frederick Dale Bruner, *The Gospel of John: A Commentary* (Grand Rapids, MI: Eerdmans, 2012), 1243–44.
3   George Müller, *The Autobiography of George Müller* (London: J. Nisbet and Co., 1906), 152.

need ministry to satisfy you. The more satisfied you are in Christ, the freer you are to give yourself to ministry without losing yourself through ministry.

Second, rejoice in being saved more than you rejoice in being significant. Dr. D. Martyn Lloyd-Jones was one of the most influential preachers of the twentieth century. Nearly forty years after his death in 1981, his fingerprints are all over the recent resurgence of Reformed theology. On July 26, 1980, Iain Murray visited Lloyd-Jones at his home in Ealing, a borough in West London.[4] For the previous two months, ill health had left Lloyd-Jones, in his own words, unable "to preach or do anything else." Here is Murray's account of their conversation that day:

> He began by speaking of how God times the encouragements He sends to us and then went on to talk of the great importance of the command which Christ gave to His disciples on witnessing their first success, "Notwithstanding in this rejoice not that the spirits are subject unto you; but rather rejoice, because your names are written in heaven" [Luke 10:20 KJV]. "Bear that in mind," he said solemnly. "Our greatest danger is to live upon our activity. The ultimate test of a preacher is what he feels like when he cannot preach." Our relationship to God is to be the supreme cause of joy. To lean upon sermons or words of testimony from others is "a real snare for all preachers." "We cannot lean on them." . . . "People say to me it must be very trying for you not to be able to preach—No! Not at all! I was not living upon preaching."

---

4   For the account that follows, see Iain Murray, *David Martyn Lloyd-Jones: The Fight of Faith 1939–1981* (Edinburgh: Banner of Truth, 1990), 737–39. The parenthetical Scripture reference in the subsequent block quote is mine.

Third, rejoice in God's work when it has nothing to do with you. In Acts 11:21, we learn that a great number of people in Antioch came to faith in the Lord Jesus. The church in Jerusalem sent Barnabas to see this work firsthand. How did Barnabas respond to this striking work of God in which he played no part? "When he came and saw the grace of God, he was glad, and he exhorted them all to remain faithful to the Lord with steadfast purpose, for he was a good man, full of the Holy Spirit and of faith" (Acts 11:23–24). Does God's grace, poured out on others through instruments other than you, gladden you?

But putting sin to death is only half the story. Ambition needs to be not only slain but also resurrected. Paul commands us not only to put off the old self but also to "put on the new self" (Eph. 4:22–24). What ambitions belong to that new self? Here is one that should be every believer's: "So whether we are at home or away, we make it our aim to please him" (2 Cor. 5:9). The Greek verb behind the phrase "we make it our aim" could be more literally translated "be ambitious." In Romans 15:20, Paul uses the same verb to name the desire that constrained the whole course of his life: "I make it my ambition to preach the gospel, not where Christ has already been named, lest I build on someone else's foundation." This ambition followed fittingly from Paul's personal commission from Christ to be apostle to the Gentiles. And, by analogy, Paul's ambition affords a model for aspiring pastors today.

What should you be ambitious for? Be ambitious to preach Christ where he is not known. Be ambitious to preach "the unsearchable riches of Christ" (Eph. 3:8). Be ambitious to bring about the obedience of faith for the sake of Christ's name among all nations (Rom. 1:5). Be ambitious for the complete maturity of everyone who confesses Christ (Col. 1:28–29). Be ambitious for godliness—your own and others' (1 Tim. 4:7–16).

The opposite of selfish ambition is not passivity but selfless ambition. The antidote to striving for your own glory is not no striving at all, but striving for God's glory. Scripture urges every Christian, "Do not be slothful in zeal, be fervent in spirit, serve the Lord" (Rom. 12:11). How can you ignite another's flame if your own is faltering?

Over the years, I have found reading the biographies and autobiographies of eminent Christians, especially pastors and missionaries, to be one of the most consistent means of kindling spiritual zeal and nurturing godly ambition. If your fire is burning low, borrow fuel from a proven source.

Slay and resurrect ambition. Selfish ambition can sabotage your ministry like a parasitic weed silently strangling each plant in your garden. But godly ambition burns clean, cleanses, and spreads.

25

Be Careful Who You Work For

So if there is any encouragement in Christ, any comfort
from love, any participation in the Spirit, any affection
and sympathy, complete my joy by being of the same mind,
having the same love, being in full accord and of one mind.

PHILIPPIANS 2:1–2

A YOUNG MAN EAGER for pastoral experience hears of a church look-ing to hire an associate pastor. The senior pastor seems likeminded. He uses the same shorthand: "Reformed," "expository preaching," "9Marks-friendly." The church seems healthy; the members are sweet and welcoming. Opportunities like this do not come along too often. The church is asking for three to five years. There is some talk of plant-ing a church at that point, hopefully by sending the associate pastor and a couple dozen members.

Would you jump at this opportunity? What questions would you ask?

When a church grows enough that they both need and can afford a second full-time pastor, they often hire an associate or assistant pastor. That pastor usually does much of what the senior pastor does, though less frequently: preaching, teaching, planning and leading services, counseling, baptizing, presiding over the Lord's Supper, and so on. The associate pastor might also give special attention to other areas of ministry, whether adult education or evangelizing youth or administration or whatever it might be.

There are lots of jobs a church might offer you. This chapter will focus on the role of associate pastor as sketched above, since it carries unique promise and pitfalls for an aspiring pastor.

The role of associate pastor combines two principles that stand in some tension: parity (or equality) and hierarchy. The associate pastor, like the senior pastor, is one of the elders. As an elder, each has only one vote. Each will sometimes lose votes and then need to submit to the will of the whole. In that sense, an associate pastor serves with and alongside the senior pastor. In an important sense, they are equals. They hold the same office. But in an equally important sense, an associate pastor serves under the senior pastor. As a general rule, whoever preaches the most has the most authority. Whoever owns the pulpit sets the direction of the church. Whatever title you give the main preacher, he will nearly always wield more authority than other elders.

This extra authority can have both informal and formal elements. Informally, people naturally look to the senior pastor for answers. His words often carry the most weight. There are many changes in the church that will not happen unless driven by the senior pastor. Formally, for a senior pastor to do his job, he must be able to act with authority in the areas of ministry for which he is responsible. It would be futile and absurd for a senior pastor to have to submit every sermon text and title, every Sunday's order of service, and every choice of a Sunday school teacher to a vote of the whole eldership.

Serving faithfully as an associate pastor means finding your place along both axes: the horizontal axis of parity and partnership, and the vertical axis of hierarchy and submission. An associate pastor is both a fellow elder and an employee, an equal and a subordinate. To be an associate pastor, you need to know when to say, "Here's what I think we should do," and when to say, "Absolutely—I'll get right on it." Your senior pastor may be your friend and mentor. He is a fellow elder. He is also your boss.

Here are four of the most common mistakes I have seen men make in becoming an associate pastor. First, accepting a call when you do not know the church, and especially the senior pastor, as well as you should. How well do you know the senior pastor's preaching, functional theology, philosophy of ministry, character, and personality? How much do you trust him? How happy are you to submit to him?

Second, underestimating philosophical differences, and how divisive those differences can be. Evaluate a senior pastor based on what he has done so far, not based on what he says he wants to do. Give far more weight to his fruit than his plans. Probe beneath the surface of common affirmations. He says he wants meaningful membership, so what does the membership process look like? He affirms plural eldership, so when is the last time he lost a vote?

Sometimes, in a spirit of deference and charity, a young man with sharp ecclesiological convictions resolves to put some of them aside to serve for a season under a godly, fruitful man of a broader mindset. If you have a long list of convictions about the church, do not work for a man whose list is shorter than yours. A preference is one thing, a conviction is another. Know the difference before you apply for a position or accept a call. In most circumstances, there is very little you can do to change a senior pastor's mind about key ecclesiological issues, especially if those changes will result in him paying new personal costs. If a church is going to tighten up its requirements for membership and raise its expectations for members, the senior pastor will pay a disproportionate amount of the relational bill. He is not going to volunteer for that pain unless his conscience compels him. And if there is little you can do to change a senior pastor's mind, there is even less you can do to change the church.

In order to be a member of a church, you need to agree with its basic teachings and practices. To serve as an elder, you must be even more likeminded, since you need to teach, endorse, and carry out those doctrinal and practical commitments. To serve as an associate pastor, the bar is even higher, since carrying out those commitments is your full-time job.

Consider not just your fit with the senior pastor but your fit with the church. How well do you mesh with its overall ethos, commitments, and culture? Unless you are becoming the senior pastor, do not work for a church that you wouldn't join if they weren't paying you to.

A third mistake is signing on to a role you don't really want. Today, it seems that more and more churches' second hire is not a generalist associate pastor, but an "administrative pastor" or "executive pastor." I appreciate that many senior pastors feel an urgent need for administrative help, but I don't like the trend. In any case, let's say you were offered a job that was 50 percent administration and 50 percent pastoring. How eagerly would you carry out the administrative half? What if half turned out to be more like three quarters? Of course, nearly every pastoral role will involve some "cost of doing business" work—email and scheduling and budgeting and expense reports and all the rest. And being flexible and willing to pick up slack is a virtue in any workplace. But consider the job description and expectations carefully before you sign on the dotted line.

Fourth, beware the vague succession plan. Many aging pastors approach retirement asymptotically: they draw continually closer but never arrive. "Come and be my associate. We'll overlap for two years, and then I'll hand it over to you and move to Florida." Unless that senior pastor has signed his name next to a retirement date, that is not a plan. What is it? It could be a hope, a whim, a pipe dream, who knows. But it isn't a plan. Decide whether to accept based on the role you are being offered, not the one you hope comes next.

Serving as an associate pastor is a delicate operation, but it can be a delight. In my own experience, one of the most important features of a healthy associate role is getting to be a generalist, as opposed to being stuck in a silo. Our church normally has five associate pastors and one or two assistant pastors—the main differences being length of tenure and length of job description. But even though we associate pastors have distinct areas of focus, we are all fundamentally generalists. All the associate pastors and assistant pastors teach publicly. We all do premarital counseling and officiate weddings. We all conduct membership interviews. From time to time, we all serve as the point person in crushingly complex pastoral cases. In a role like the one I am privileged to serve in, being an associate pastor gives you the opportunity to learn by experience on someone else's—that is, the senior pastor's—relational dime.

The more an associate pastor's work is like a senior pastor's, the better training it will be. The senior pastor I serve with (and under!), Mark Dever, has a genius for this. I benefit daily from the way he has crafted my role to serve not only the church but also me. Mark preaches about twenty-five or thirty Sunday mornings each year, and I preach twelve or fourteen. Over time, I have taken on the bulk of our Wednesday night Bible studies. My role also involves moderating members' meetings, supervising younger staff members, leading the staff when Mark is away, overseeing our internship, and helping facilitate church planting and revitalizing. All these are ways my position is set up to advance not just the church's ministry but, Lord willing, also my future work as a senior pastor. Senior pastors, take note. Craft an associate role not only to benefit your members, but to equip a pastor who will go somewhere you can't: the future.

26

Candidate Candidly

But we have renounced disgraceful, underhanded ways. We
refuse to practice cunning or to tamper with God's word,
but by the open statement of the truth we would commend
ourselves to everyone's conscience in the sight of God.

2 CORINTHIANS 4:2

HOW SHOULD YOU APPROACH the process by which a church
decides whether to call you as their pastor? The only pastoral candidacy I have undergone was decidedly atypical. So, in this chapter,
I assemble and adapt advice from friends whose experiences might
more closely preview yours.[1]

Among the churches I am most familiar with, a pastoral search
usually goes something like this: A senior pastor leaves or announces
that he is leaving soon. The church then delegates the process of
selecting a pastoral candidate to a "search committee." This search
committee might include a couple of elders or staff members. Most
members of the committee will likely be selected to represent some

---

1 Special thanks to Eric Bancroft, Blake Boylston, Noah Braymen, Bret Capranica,
Nathan Carter, Garrett Conner, Caleb Greggson, and Marc Minter.

of the church's demographics or—I hate to say it—interest groups. These half-dozen or so brothers and sisters then might collect and vet dozens or even hundreds of résumés. They winnow the stack to a short list, and then listen to sample sermons, contact references, and perhaps conduct a phone interview with each candidate. Eventually, they settle on one candidate and inform the congregation. A visit or series of visits ensues. The candidate usually meets with key leaders and groups of members, answers a long stream of questions, and preaches "in view of a call." If all goes well, the church votes to call him shortly after.

To put it gently, there are many ways this typical process could be improved.[2] But this chapter is not for the church or the search committee; it's for you. So, if you are faced with a process like this, how should you conduct yourself?

Be candid. A pastoral candidacy is like dating. Both parties put their best foot forward; both tend to be on their best behavior. An element of this is inevitable, but the pressures on both sides can push against transparency and even integrity. Imagine you have made it through the first round or two, and a search committee is interviewing you by phone. What would they like least about your theological convictions and ministry philosophy if only they had the cleverness to ask? Don't wait for them to ask; tell them yourself.

---

2 See, for instance, Mark Dever's message on how to find a pastor at the 9Marks at SEBTS conference in 2017, available at https://www.9marks.org/message/leadership -mark-dever-session-1-9marks-at-southeastern-2017/; accessed June 23, 2020. See further Mark's pair of articles "What's Wrong With Search Committees? Part 1 of 2 on Finding a Pastor," 9Marks, December 20, 2010, https://www.9marks.org /article/whats-wrong-search-committees-part-1-2-finding-pastor/, and "What's Right About Elders? Part 2 of 2 on Finding a Pastor," 9Marks, December 20, 2010, https://www.9marks.org/article/whats-right-about-elders-part-2-2-finding-pastor/.

Before you are faced with the decision of accepting or rejecting their call, know your non-negotiables. What hills would you die on? What could you live with, whether for a while or for four decades? Would you accept a call if the church is egalitarian by default but not design? Would you accept if the church's services regularly conclude with altar calls and they expect that practice to continue?

Be prepared for barrages of questions. Sometimes you might want to ask a clarifying question of your own before you answer. Does your questioner mean the same thing by "Calvinism" that you do? Is there a question behind the question? Make sure you know what the question is before you answer it. "If one gives an answer before he hears, it is his folly and shame" (Prov. 18:13).

Pastor them in the search process. Even if they decide not to call you as their pastor, you might help that search committee do their job better. Most search committees are staffed by sweet, sincere men and women who are sacrificially giving time and energy to help their church make a momentous decision. These are not just sheep without a shepherd; they are sheep trying to select a shepherd. They are not necessarily well-equipped for the task. Love them. Care for them. Pray that they will choose wisely. And, to whatever extent you are able, help them see and focus on what is most important in a pastor.

Seek clarity about expectations and responsibilities. Articulate what you understand the responsibilities of a pastor to include. Do you understand every element of the church's public services to be a ministry of the word, and therefore finally the responsibility of the elders? (Ahem: you should.) If so, what if the church has a full-time worship leader who is used to having final say over everything in the service but the sermon? Further, whether you are applying for a senior pastorate or an associate role, burrow into specifics about the church's expectations of you, your job description, and your weekly schedule. Does the church gladly affirm the centrality of expository preaching, and therefore the costly priority of time spent preparing to preach? Are you expected to be present for every program? Sit on every committee? Visit every member who falls ill? If so, when do they expect you to prepare sermons, not to mention lead your family?

Remember that they're not just interviewing you; you're interviewing them. Candidating goes both ways. Once the search process has got far enough, ask the committee when it might be appropriate for you to ask them a series of questions. Your questionnaire might include, among much else, their understanding of preaching and its importance; their philosophy of corporate worship and how they decide which songs to sing; their approach to sending and supporting missionaries; their practice of counseling and its relation to psychology; and their practices, if any, of church membership and discipline.

Rather than asking questions that announce themselves by ringing the doorbell of standard vocabulary, you will likely learn more by asking questions that slip in a side door. So, especially in face-to-face conversation, instead of asking about "church membership" you might ask, Do you know if, in the past few years, anyone who applied for membership has been denied? Instead of asking about church discipline, ask, Without telling me names or details, can you think of any church member who was confronted by another church member for engaging in sexual immorality? What was the result? Instead of asking about evangelism and discipleship, you could ask, Can you tell me about an adult convert in the church who came to faith recently? How are they doing? Is anyone regularly spending time with them to help them learn to pray and read their Bible?

Try to gain a three-dimensional view of the church. Ask about who makes decisions and how leaders are chosen. Try to spot unofficial power pockets. Ask to see the church's budget and financial statements, and ask about their practices of financial accountability. Get to know the church's history and reputation in the community. Seek second opinions from people who are outside the church but nearby. That could mean people who are not currently members but who grew up in the church, or other pastors in the area whom you trust. While the search committee should be primarily concerned with your character, convictions, and competence, your assessment of the church should include culture and chemistry.

Candidating is an uncertain process. It can also be uncomfortable, even unnerving. A clear conscience is a soft pillow, and God's sovereignty is an even softer one. Candidate candidly, and trust your loving heavenly Father to direct your steps and provide for his people.

27

Cherish Christ

Indeed, I count everything as loss because of the
surpassing worth of knowing Christ Jesus my Lord.
PHILIPPIANS 3:8

THERE ARE TWO KINDS of comparisons.

One, you can say how good something is by saying how bad something else is. I have no stake in any debates over sports or the teams that play them. So, rest assured, the following example is purely hypothetical. "Golf? That isn't even a sport. You drive around in a cart for four hours, occasionally stepping out to whack a tiny ball. I could get more exercise washing the dishes. Now basketball, there's a real sport."

Two, you can say how good something is by saying how much better it is than something else that's already really good. "Okay, imagine the best dish you've ever eaten, then multiply that by twenty-five tiny courses, one after the other for three hours, each as good as the last."

Throughout this book, I have mainly tried to shake you down. Slow you down. Rough you up. Stretch you. Help you find pressure points and blind spots. I have assumed zeal for ministry and have sought to add knowledge. I have assumed desire for the work and have sought to help you qualify for the work. Accordingly, I have not said much about the glories of pastoral ministry. But boy is it glorious. As so often, Spurgeon said it better than I could hope to:

> I would sooner have my work to do than any other under the sun. Preaching Jesus Christ is sweet work, joyful work, Heavenly work. Whitefield used to call his pulpit his throne, and those who know the bliss of forgetting everything beside the glorious, all-absorbing topic of Christ crucified, will bear witness that the term was aptly used. It is a bath in the waters of Paradise to preach with the Holy Ghost sent down from Heaven. Scarcely is it possible for a man, this side the grave, to be nearer Heaven than is a preacher when his Master's presence bears him right away from every care and thought, save the one business in hand, and that the greatest that ever occupied a creature's mind and heart.[1]

Robert Murray M'Cheyne once realized while preaching, "It came across me in the pulpit, that if spared to be a minister, I might enjoy sweet flashes of communion with God in that situation."[2]

Have you tasted that bliss? Taken that bath? Enjoyed those sweet flashes of communion with God? If you have, you know that, in addition to hard work and heartache, pastoral ministry serves up rare joys. The pleasures of pastoral ministry can be so rich that you are tempted to want them too much.

---

1   C. H. Spurgeon, *Autobiography: Volume 1: The Early Years, 1834–1859; a revised edition, originally compiled by Susannah Spurgeon and Joseph Harrald* (Edinburgh: Banner of Truth, 1962), 403–4.

2   Andrew A. Bonar, *Memoir and Remains of Robert Murray M'Cheyne* (Edinburgh: Banner of Truth, 1966), 33.

So here is my parting word: cherish Christ. As good as pastoral ministry is, Jesus is infinitely better. The risen, exalted, soon-returning Christ proclaims to his waiting, suffering, longing people, "I am the Alpha and the Omega, the first and the last, the beginning and the end" (Rev. 22:13). Christ is the beginning and the end of pastoral ministry. He is the beginning and end of your relationship with God. He is the beginning and end of your life. He is the beginning and end of the universe. Cherish him more than you cherish serving him. Cherish him more than you cherish telling others about him. Cherish him more than you cherish leading his people. Cherish Christ. "For to me to live is Christ" (Phil. 1:21).

Few living men whom I have met embody this better than Ray Ortlund Jr., who recently retired from pastoring Immanuel Nashville. Ray is the son of a godly man and the father of godly men. He learned to cherish Christ from his father and has taught his children to cherish Christ. The last words of this book will be the last words that Ray Ortlund Sr. had for his son:

Early on Sunday, July 22, 2007, my dad woke up in his hospital room in Newport Beach. He knew it was finally his day of release from this life. He had the nurse call the family in. My wife, Jani, and I were far away in Ireland for ministry that day. We didn't know what was happening back home. But the family gathered at dad's bedside. They read Scripture. They sang hymns. Dad spoke a word of patriarchal blessing and admonition to each one, a message suited to encourage and guide. He pronounced over them all the blessing of Aaron: "The Lord bless you and keep you; the Lord make his face to shine upon you and be gracious to you; the Lord lift up his countenance upon you and give you peace" (Numbers 6:24–26).

And then, quietly, he fell asleep.

Later I asked my sister about dad's message to me. It was this: "Tell Bud, ministry isn't everything. Jesus is."[3]

3   Ray Ortlund, "10 Unforgettable Lessons On Fatherhood," Desiring God, May 16, 2015, https://www.desiringgod.org/articles/10-unforgettable-lessons-on-fatherhood.

General Index

Scripture Index

9Marks

Building Healthy Churches

9Marks exists to equip church leaders with a biblical vision and practical resources for displaying God's glory to the nations through healthy churches.

To that end, we want to see churches characterized by these nine marks of health:

1. Expositional Preaching
2. Gospel Doctrine
3. A Biblical Understanding of Conversion and Evangelism
4. Biblical Church Membership
5. Biblical Church Discipline
6. A Biblical Concern for Discipleship and Growth
7. Biblical Church Leadership
8. A Biblical Understanding of the Practice of Prayer
9. A Biblical Understanding and Practice of Missions

Find all our Crossway titles and other resources at 9Marks.org.